HONDA/ACURA

Driver/Owner Guide
1962-1990

G. William Krause

Motorbooks International
Publishers & Wholesalers

To my Dad

For sharing his love, knowledge and appreciation of cars with me, and for his encouragement and enthusiasm that helped make this book possible.

First published in 1990 by Motorbooks International Publishers & Wholesalers P O Box 2, 729 Prospect Avenue, Osceola, WI 54020 USA

Library of Congress Cataloging-in-Publication Data
Krause, G. William
    Honda/Acura driver/owner guide / G. William Krause.
      p.   cm.
    ISBN 0-87938-402-6
    1. Honda automobile—Handbooks. manuals, etc.   2. Acura
automobile—Handbooks, manuals, etc.   I. Title.
TL215.H58K73   1990   89-13280
629.222′2—dc20   CIP

On the front cover: A hot yellow 1989 CRX Si, photographed in Eden Prairie, Minnesota. *G. William Krause*

Printed and bound in the United States of America

Contents

Acknowledgments

A special thanks to the following people and companies for giving me their time and for sharing their information on Hondas past, present and future. Dave is one in a million, and Michael, Barbara and Tim were incredibly patient and helpful.

Dave Jenkins
American Honda Motor Company
Jackson Racing
King Motorsports (Mugen)
Road & Track
Michael Dregni
Barbara Harold
Tim Parker
Hopkins Honda
Bloomington Acura
Chris Wallwork
Jim Dentici

Introduction

No team in the history of Formula One racing has dominated a season the way the Honda-powered McLarens did in 1988. The McLaren-Hondas won fifteen of the sixteen Grands Prix of the year, and drivers Ayrton Senna and Alain Prost finished first and second in ten of those races. Senna won the world championship and a record eight races while teammate Prost chalked up an unprecedented 105 points. Obviously, the constructors world championship also went to McLaren-Honda in 1988.

Honda's success came as no surprise. Honda has been building Formula One engines since the mid-sixties; however, success did not come until the eighties. In fact, it was a Honda engine that helped Nelson Piquet capture the world crown in 1987 as well as the constructors title for the Williams-Honda team.

Honda's first F1 engine did receive considerable attention. The car premiered in the 1964 German Grand Prix. It had a 215 bhp V-12 with transistorized ignition and twelve carburetors. Indirect fuel injection replaced the carburetors in 1965, and Richie Ginther drove it to first place in the Mexican Grand Prix. That was the last year of the 1.5 liter formulas, but the first big step for Honda engineering—and an incredible venture for a motorcycle manufacturer.

The three words say it all: Powered by Honda. Ayrton Senna's Formula One world champion McLaren/Honda. Senna, teammate Alain Prost and their turbo V-6 Honda-powered cars combined for a record fifteen wins and fifteen pole positions.

Of course, Senna and Prost's 700 bhp, turbo V-6 differs greatly from the engine in your Honda, but it is this racing history and technology that put Honda cars on the leading edge of design and engineering.

This is a remarkable achievement when you consider that Honda has been building automobiles for just twenty-five years. Honda began producing motorcycles in 1948 and quickly mastered the art of the small four-stroke engine. Using this knowledge, it debuted a small sports car in 1962, the 360. It was a stubby, two-seat convertible that some say had awkward styling. I think it is an attractive car resembling the MGB.

The S360 and its brothers, the S500, S600 and S800, were unique and technologically advanced cars for their day. However, they still contained basic principles of motorcycle technology: they had one single-barrel carburetor per cylinder and a two-chain rear drive. The most incredible thing about these cars was their high-revving engines. For example, peak horsepower came at 8,500 rpm with a redline of 11,000 rpm. Consider that in comparison with today's high-tech CRX that hits red at a hair over six grand.

While the S600 and S800 were being developed, Honda introduced a car more akin to the Civics we know and love: the N360, debuting in 1966. It was powered by a 354 cc twin-cylinder, air-cooled engine with the drive wheels up front. It even looked like a miniaturized Civic with squared corners and tiny wheels.

The N360 was only available in the home market; a bored-out 500 cc version was built for export. These early front-drivers were soon replaced by the N400 and N600. The N600 was the first Honda to reach American shores four years after it was conceived. The S-Types were never available in the United States, but a number have found their way to American soil.

Much has changed since those first 600 models. In just eighteen years, we have gone from small cars with simplistic styling powered by Honda's respected motorcycle engines to state-of-the-art cars featuring an excellent combination of economics and ergonomics.

Honda cars offer a little something for everybody with the end result being the same—plenty of smiles per hour. I have yet to meet a Honda owner who has not been pleased with his or her car. In fact, most Honda drivers own or have owned at least two models. Take a minute to think of the number of Honda cars in your neighborhood and the number of two-Honda families you know. Five Hondas park on my block alone.

What is it about these cars that makes them so popular? For one thing, they are almost like a fine appliance. Hondas seem to run long and strong with minimal maintenance and still deliver excellent fuel economy. Most Honda owners take it as a personal affront if their cars need to go to the repair shop.

Even the media cannot say enough about the cars. Honda has captured three Import Car of the Year honors from *Motor Trend*, including two clean sweeps of the top three spots. The Civic was Car of the Year in 1980; the CRX, Prelude and Civic S took the top three places in 1984; 1988 saw the CRX Si, Civic sedan and Prelude Si 4WS in the top slots. Honda has also achieved the highest EPA mileage rating in the world three times, even surpassing diesels. If Hondas are so perfect, then why doesn't everybody drive one? And, above all, why write a book?

Well, as a fellow Honda driver—I'm on my second—I have discovered nothing in print for us Honda/Acura lovers to have, hold and learn from. It is important to understand how we got to the CRX from the S360 through the history of Honda cars and their engineering. Above all, I want to show you how you can enjoy your car even more. Yes, believe it or not, the cars can be improved in several areas, including parts and accessories. I also give driving tips for street and competition.

This book primarily focuses on the CRX and Integra. I have included the entire range of S-Types, Civics, Accords and Preludes since little information on them is available and they are equally important players in Honda's history.

The CRX has been lauded as one of the best all-around two-seaters on the road today. Since its debut in 1984, the Civic/CRX, nicknamed the "Egg" among other things, has featured excellent performance, economy and comfort.

I cannot count the number of times some highway hero has challenged me and my CRX Si to a stoplight duel thanks to all this positive press. I'm sure the same has happened to you. Sometimes you bite and sometimes you don't; a lot depends on the other car and the circumstances. Obviously, we won't go head-to-head with a Corvette or IROC-Z Camaro—which would be like challenging Mike Tyson to a fistfight—but we can always have some fun with MR2s, Fieros, Escort GTs, Celicas and the like. I hate to inflate their egos, but VW GTIs are tough adversaries.

If you have had your CRX for any length of time, you are probably as tired of being baited as I am. The performance of the 1.5 liter CRXs was once one of the best-kept secrets in the automotive field. The car's power and nimble handling allowed amateur drivers to compete successfully in autocross events and aggravated owners of many other pricey sports cars on the street. Unfortunately, the secret got out all too soon. The CRX has now been bumped up several classes in autocross and has fared well on the Pro-Solo circuits.

I have found the CRX to be an excellent cruising and commuting car. Far from a grand touring car mind you, but nothing can beat a warm sunny day with the windows down, the roof open and miles of twisting blacktop in front of you. Some of the most fun I have had with the car is discovering what it can do. I was not even able to drive a CRX before I purchased one. Oddly enough, many Honda drivers have only gotten to sit in a car similar to the one they wanted or, worse, only got to look at pictures.

Learning the secrets of the car was a joy. From the day I took delivery, I have been continually surprised by the car's performance; the power and handling can make winding roads a delight, but you have probably also gotten in a little over your head at times. Once I was challenging a cloverleaf at 70 mph and suddenly found myself spinning through the infield. No damage beyond a cloud of dust in the air and a bruised ego, fortunately. It should come as no surprise that a few piled-up CRXs rest in boneyards, so we will explore the car's handling and fast driving. We will also look at why the CRX is considered a sports car and why your insurance is so high.

Chapter 1

S Series

Prelude to the invasion

Today we regard the CRX and Prelude as economy sports cars. Many people feel this is a new dimension in the car market and especially a new venture for Honda. After all, Honda is perceived to primarily build family-oriented economy cars.

In reality, Honda's first production car was a sports car. The two-seat convertible S360 of 1962 was a technical marvel, yet in its styling the car was not as sleek, sexy or refined as other sports cars of that time. Consider that the Jaguar E-Type and the Ferrari 250GT California debuted at about the same time.

The S360 was followed by the S500, S600, S800 and S800 coupe, which were refined versions of the original design with bored-out en-

The first Honda truck, the T360, powered by the 360 cc engine. This was the forerunner of the S Series sports cars, *as the high-revving motor served as the powerplant for Honda's first car.* Christopher Wallwork

gines. The cars were simple yet complex with unique and innovative elements, not unlike today's Hondas.

These first Hondas are rare and somewhat exotic, especially in the United States as they were never officially imported here. The S800 does not have the renown of a Ferrari but it does rank with the hot Mini Cooper S. Keep in mind that if you plan to purchase one of these cars as an investment you will have to sit on it for quite a while before it becomes valuable.

History

Honda's car building began in the early 1960s at the same time as Honda was enjoying tremendous success and notoriety with its racing motorcycles. In 1962, founder Soichiro Honda assembled a design team to come up with a vehicle that was sports minded yet also fell within the lower bracket of Japan's sky-high insurance premiums. The result was the two-seat convertible sports car dubbed the S360. The engine came from the T360 truck built during the same period.

There are conflicting reports as to which was the first car produced by Honda, the S360 or S500. The T360 truck debuted at the same time and all sources agree that the engine for the first car came from the truck, which leads me to believe the S360 was Honda's first automobile while the S500 came soon after.

Honda's mastery of the small four-stroke engine had brought it international renown, and the company fully used this technology in the S360. The S360 was powered by a 356 cc four-cylinder engine with two twin-choke Keihin carburetors. The engine also had a light alloy head, twin chain-driven camshafts and a roller bearing crankshaft. Capping off the S360's motorcycle origins was the two-chain, independently sprung final drive—one chain for each driving wheel. This little engine was capable of incredibly high rpm and produced its peak of 33 horsepower at 9000

A future collectible? The 1965 Honda S600 sports car powered by a 600 cc engine and rear chain drive. The engine was a bored-out version of the original 360 cc motor. Asking prices for Honda's S Series have been climbing steadily, but they are still reasonable. The cars are much harder to find in the United States since they were never officially imported. Road & Track

11

rpm for a top speed of 85 mph. The power was harnessed by four-wheel aluminum drum brakes.

The styling was aggressive but as with all early Hondas, a bit choppy. The back end stopped too soon and appeared square when seen from the rear. Two oversized taillights and a large license plate light cluttered up the rear-most panel. The car was most attractive in profile, yet it still looked a bit confining, much like the Austin-Healey Bugeye Sprite.

The short, sloping hood featured a small, oblong bulge on the right side of the car to make room for the carburetors' airbox. The grille had an oval mouth with turn indicators incorporated into the trim and single round headlights outboard.

In the cockpit, you got a sporty feel with two bucket seats providing good lateral support, and beyond the wood-trimmed steering wheel was a simple but handsome dashboard. A large 200 km/h speedometer and 11,000 rpm tachometer were mounted directly ahead of the driver with two smaller circular gauges off to the right. One monitored the coolant temperature while the other was shared by fuel and voltage gauges. Below these two dials were pull levers for the choke, headlights and wipers. Of interest was the toggle lever mounted on the fascia which operated the horn; the horn sounded as the lever was moved up or down, the theory being that the driver's hands would not have to leave the wheel to operate the horn. The headlamp dimmer switch, of the same design, was on the other side of the wheel.

The door panels were plain contourless vinyl with only the door handle and window roll-ups for decoration. A four-speed stick rose from the center of the squared-off tunnel.

The car was indeed small. Overall length was just 131.3 inches with a 78.7 inch wheelbase. It was just fifty-five inches from side to side and

The cockpit of the S Series delivers everything a sports car should: a full complement of gauges, readily accessible controls and a shift lever that falls into your hand. Note the size of the AM/FM radio at the lower center of the dash. Pictured is an S600. Road & Track

Coupe and convertible versions of the S600 side by side. Note the aluminum-alloy wheels and different mounting positions for the mirrors. Christopher Wallwork

only 47.8 inches high with a total curb weight of 1,556 lb. Compare this to a Sprite with an eighty-inch wheelbase, overall length of 137.5 inches and 1,600 lb. weight.

The car used a basic ladder frame with tubular cross-members. Independent suspension was standard all the way around, with a torsion bar up front. The car was guided by rack-and-pinion steering with just 2½ turns lock to lock. Dunlop radial-ply tubed tires were fitted to thirteen-inch stamped steel rims.

The original formula was good, so naturally the next thing to do was beef up the power and make the car more marketable in the rest of the world.

In 1963 Honda increased the displacement to 531 cc and introduced the S500 which boasted 44 bhp at 8,000 rpm for a top speed of 90 mph. Everything from the S360 remained the same including the chain drive, independent suspension and drum brakes.

Front and rear views of the S800. Looking at the car from the front gives the feeling of a sleek, rounded design; viewing the car from the rear renders a stubby, square, choppy look. Note the small-diameter dual exhaust pipes.

13

All models were convertibles until the debut of the S600 in the spring of 1964. Honda had increased the displacement again pushing power output to 57 bhp and it added a coupe model. The coupe was virtually the same except for a long, rounded hardtop that ran from the windshield to the rear of the car, similar in appearance to a miniature Triumph GT6. The extra sheet metal only added forty-three pounds to the car.

Keep in mind that these were primarily produced for the Japanese homeland and were not randomly produced specials. A few cars appeared in other countries but production numbers were low until the S600 debuted. In 1964 Honda built 5,210 S600s and 8,779 units in 1965. The S600 was also sold in other right-hand-drive countries such as Australia and England. Shortly after that Honda offered left-hand-drive cars for other markets.

S800

The popularity of the S-Type Honda was on the rise after early sluggish sales but the car still could not compete with Sprites and Midgets. Thus in 1966 Honda introduced the new S800. Displacement was increased to 791 cc which resulted in 70 bhp at 8,000 rpm for a top speed of 100 mph. Initially Honda kept the running gear intact but early in the life of the S800 Honda gave the car a live rear axle, replacing the dual chain drive, and front disc brakes.

The new rear suspension included radius rods, coil springs and hydraulic dampers. This change came early in 1966 and thus makes the chain drive S800s rare. This also marked the difference between a Mk.1 S800 and a Mk.2 S800.

The Mk.2 version became popular in just about every market in the world except America. This was the market Honda wanted to capitalize on; after all, Americans bought MGs, Triumphs, Jaguars and Austin-Healeys by the boatload. The S800 should fit right in.

An excellent profile shot of the S800 coupe. Entry and exit were encumbered by the small doors and sills. The large steering wheel also interfered with the driver. The ground clearance was high for such a small car.

14

Unfortunately one thing stood between the S800 and the US market: American safety legislation. The car did not measure up in many ways so Honda made changes including flush door handles, side marker lights, hazard lights, dual circuit brakes and more. All this was for naught because the marvelous little high-revving engine was guilty of emitting too many hydrocarbons. Without the support of the American market Honda ceased S800 production in early 1970.

Had the car reached the American market it could have been a fine seller. In 1968 an S800 could have been bought for just 800 pounds sterling, approximately $1,200 US. A large number of S-Type Hondas were built and many still exist. Production figures are as follows: 1,363 S500 (1963–64); 13,034 S600 (1964–67); and 11,406 S800 (1966–70).

A number of S800s have found their way onto American soil but finding one can be difficult. Keep your eye on the enthusiast publications. If you have to find one you can contact the Honda S800 Sports Car Club in England listed in the back of the book.

Driving

The S800 was quite quick for its day. Only 13.5 seconds separated the S800 from rest and 60 mph, and it covered a quarter-mile in 18.8 seconds. That equaled the performance of an MGB of the same era. In a 1967 road test, *Autocar* magazine called the S800 the "fastest one-liter car in the world." The S800 also emitted a howling noise from its dual exhausts that made bystanders take notice.

Sitting in the S800 makes you appreciate curb height as you sit so low to the ground. If the car had the cutaway doors popular in the 1950s, you could drag your knuckles on the road.

The cockpit is somewhat cramped. The seats do move forward and backward easily but not enough for long-legged drivers. Remember, wheelbase on the S-Types was 1.3 inches shorter than on an MG Midget. The seat cushions are springy, a bit coarse feeling and short on thigh support. The seatbacks are firm with hardly any lateral support and no rake adjustment.

A look under the hood revealed the high-revving S800 powerplant. In plain view are the four individual carburetors and the large airbox that fed them. The obvious tight fit of the 800 cc engine emphasizes the car's small size.

Understeering in the S800. Here you can see the weight transfer toward the outboard side of the car, the tremendous stress put upon the outer front wheel and the lack of downforce on the inner wheels. The inboard front tire will soon give way, and the driver will have to keep turning into the corner to keep his line.

15

Visibility is good, and you get true vintage sports car feel as you look out over the rounded fender tops, crowned with chrome beading. The small bump on the hood adds an extra touch of raciness similar to that of the Sunbeam Alpine and Opel GT.

The attractive but large fifteen-inch steering wheel will interfere with your legs if you are tossing the car through corners. The pedals are small and placed close together in the tight footwell area, much like in a British sports car. They are also mounted slightly outward from the transmission tunnel. The close proximity of the brake and accelerator make heel-toeing, or in this case toe-toeing, easy. A firm squeeze on the brake and a quick rock of your foot will get the revs up for the downshift.

This technique is especially handy as several road tests found the synchros slow and ineffective on quick shifts. In a 1967 test of the S800, *Motor Sport* magazine said the gearbox "action is a bit notchy and synchromesh can very definitely become non-existent when snapping from third into second." Yet the testers also said that gear selection was precise.

Gearbox aside, the S-Type Hondas were well received by auto testers. The most common complaints referred to the car's smallness. Long trips were made difficult because of the tight driving quarters and lack of room for luggage. *Autocar* recommended "squashy" luggage.

Drivability of the car was reported to be good. The engine spun willingly all the way to 8500 rpm, with power coming on at 3000 rpm and the real surge above 6000 rpm. Suspension was stiff with a harsh ride suited to spirited driving.

The largest complaints came in regard to rough road surfaces. The rigid rear axle transmitted every bump through the car with a great deal

The ergonomics of the S Series dashboard was as good as any sports car of its era. The instruments were clean and simple, reminiscent of British sports cars of the same vintage. The three-spoked steering wheel with its imitation wood rim looked out of place, and its diameter was too large for the confining cockpit.

The dash display of an S800 coupe was the same as the convertible. The horn toggle is visible at the right of the wheel. This model is equipped with optional locking steering, which was separate from the ignition switch.

16

A race-prepped S600 complete with air dam lies in waiting at the Suzuka circuit in Japan. Christopher Wallwork

of commotion and rattling. Worse was the playback in the steering wheel which *Motor Sport* termed "vicious," and the testers observed constant wheel rock that resulted from the short wheelbase.

Both road testers found the S800 and its Dunlop SP3 tubed tires to have impressive grip in all conditions. Steering was said to be direct and responsive with mild understeer reported in almost all situations. *Autocar* found the understeer in sharp turns could be eliminated by throwing the car toward the apex early in the corner. On sweeping turns, the tail did not drift to the outside.

Most noticeable in driving the S800 were the engine revs and sound. In order to get the best performance from the little four-banger, you needed to use all the rev band. *Autocar* said, "Limiting revs to 6500 allows rapid motoring with the minimum of fuss and little noise." Above that mark the magazine noted that the engine sighs with all the noises and sweetness of a racing unit. *Motor Sport* called it a "splendid yowl."

Getting good power from the car not only required using the full rev band even beyond the redline but also a lot of shifting. The two road testers quoted found the gear ratios to be excellent and well-spaced.

Conclusion

All in all, the S-Type Hondas were exciting and sophisticated cars that deserve a special part in the history of Honda automobiles. It is interesting that Honda built such an advanced car right up until 1970, then began to deliver the basic air-cooled 600 to the United States—a car with ten-year-old technology.

Unlike Toyota's remarkable 2000GT, enough S-Types were manufactured so that the world could and still can enjoy them. If you do find one, keep in mind that your local Honda dealer will not service the car; he or she may not even know what it is. You will have to inquire at a sports car shop that specializes in cars like MGs and Austin-Healeys. Parts can also be difficult to find; however, the S800 club has a good handle on replacement parts and technical tips.

If ever there was a landmark Honda automobile, the S800 is it: almost a timeless body style, albeit small, and an incredible high-revving powerplant that loves to be driven. The S800 is truly the most unique Honda to own, and potentially the most valuable.

Chapter 2

Civic
The little car that could

Honda's success formula did not call for dramatic changes or new models each year. At many branchings in Honda's family tree, changes were hardly detectable if they happened at all. Honda's advertising slogan for so many years claimed "We make it simple." They did, they do and it works.

Civic predecessors

The interesting little S models never made it across the ocean to the United States. The first car that was officially imported to US soil by American Honda Motor Company was the Honda 600 two-door sedan. The car came ashore in the fall of 1969 as a 1970 model, when new cars were introduced but once a year.

The 600 was not a new car: it was four years old; it was Honda's N360 with a different engine displacement. About the time Honda was introducing the S800, the N360 was delivered to the Japanese market. It was a chunky little two-door sedan that at first glance is the obvious predecessor to the Civic.

The little front-drive car derived its name from the 354 cc twin-cylinder powerplant. It was a single-overhead-cam unit, most notable because it was air-cooled—an obvious reminder of the car's motorcycle heritage.

Honda's first car was the two-cylinder, air-cooled N360, seen here in Japan.
Christopher Wallwork

Another view of the tiny N360. Note the obtrusive rear leaf spring mounts.
Christopher Wallwork

19

The tiny twin pumped out 31 hp at 8500 rpm and had a top speed of 71 mph. The standard gearbox was a four-speed, but interestingly enough, a three-speed automatic with torque converter was also available. The stubby little car looked like a hatchback but in fact only had a small trunk in the rear. The trunk was so small the full-size, ten-inch spare tire had to be housed under the hood—but no matter, the engine did not take up much of the space. Up front was the tandem two-cylinder, air-cooled engine fed by a single carburetor. The battery and jack were secured on the left.

Equally stark was the interior. Two bench-like, vinyl-covered chairs and minimal trim decorated the insides. The dashboard was also featureless with only a speedometer, fuel gauge and radio. Coming up from under the center of the dash was the shift lever for the four-speed gearbox.

Underneath, the 360 was a simple ladder frame chassis, and at the back were two independently sprung drive-chain cases that transmitted the 31 hp to the wheels.

Akin to the 360 car was the Honda T360 that came as a small pickup or a commercial van. The only similarity was in the engine displacement. The T360 was a twin-cam, four-cylinder, water-cooled engine featuring two twin-choke carburetors, aluminum head and a roller bearing balanced crankshaft. This crankshaft design was very common in motorcycles and was designed to act as the flywheel as well. This engine was the basis for the first S360.

The N360 was only sold in Japan. Soon after it debuted, a bored-out 500 cc, 40 hp version was built for export. By 1968, the N360 and N500 were replaced by the N400 and N600 respectively. Neither of these two models had much performance over the earlier cars. The 400 cc version produced 33 hp at 8000 rpm, while the larger 598 cc engine only made 45 hp at 7000 revs.

Through this entire range of cars, the only difference was the engine displacement. The cars were small with a full-length measurement of just ten feet. This short wheelbase accounted for the cars' stiff and sometimes harsh ride. In a July 1969 extended use test, *Autocar* found the

The interior of the N360 was simple and functional. This model had a speedometer, fuel gauge, radio and vent lever. The owner has covered the bare floors with carpet. Christopher Wallwork

The small 360 cc air-cooled engine is almost dwarfed by the spare tire. A complex air intake channels air into the single carburetor. Christopher Wallwork

N600 to have a firm ride with "plenty of road roar and bump thump." The testers also pointed out that even small bumps could deflect the Honda from its course.

Styling of the N600 can best be summed up as typically 1970s Japanese. The car was short, which was accentuated by the brief hood and abrupt tail. The doors and side windows seemed too large for the rest of the car. The little ten-inch tires only helped to make the car appear smaller.

The inside was remarkably roomy in appearance. Up front were two individual seats and in the rear a bench seat. The dashboard was fairly flat, but there was little room for anything else. There was a small, cubby compartment on the passenger side, and a rectangle in front of the driver contained the speedometer and a gauge for the 6.9 gallon fuel tank. The oddest element of the dash was the stick-shift lever. It was a simple L-shaped lever that came straight out of the center of the dash. You might think shifting was awkward and clumsy, yet the up-and-down motion was surprisingly crisp. A center-mounted stick was not unique to Honda; both Renault and Citroen had similar arrangements, but theirs were not as precise.

Two views of America's first Honda automobile, the 1970 600. The most interesting feature—or nonfeature—is *that, although it looked like a hatchback, the rear did not open.* Honda

Interior trim on the original 600 Series was as basic as the design. The door trim was plain vinyl with painted metal above and below.

One unique feature in the early 600s was this roof console featuring a swiveling map light and dome light switch.

The folks at *Autocar* found the little Honda charming and endearing even though it had several shortcomings. One shortcoming was that lack of synchromesh in the gearbox. The testers complained of a perpetual and unavoidable crunch between shifts due to the constant drag. "Quick upward changes produce a grunt from the box, and very quick ones on acceleration runs, a bang." This could be avoided by pausing between up- and downshifts or by double-clutching.

Somehow *Autocar* even found fun in this when combined with the howl of the little motor. "You can make remarkable noises rushing up to things in a storm of very rackety changing-down which reduces both driver and passenger to hysterical giggles." It was quite easy to make a lot of noise and vibration by simply pressing your foot to the floor.

Sixty mph came up on the clock in 18.5 seconds, which may not seem that quick but was equal to the performance of the 988 cc Mini Cooper. *Autocar* pointed out that this was not achieved quietly. "Driving at all quickly in the Honda is like sharing a corrugated iron garden shed with the mechanical clatter of a healthy English 650 twin motorbike."

On a more serious note, *Autocar* recorded serious problems with the brakes. The front-heavy car ate up front linings in a hurry. Brake-fade and vibration were also problems.

The car also had some roadholding deficiencies. The N600 had an "appreciable" amount of bodyroll unlike the similar but lower-slung Mini. *Autocar* complained that the Dunlop C41 cross-ply tires handled marginally in the dry and were miserable in the rain, stating it was easy to lose the front end. The testers experimented with Michelin ZX tires and found a vast improvement, but steering problems still existed. "The steering is a paradox, kicking back appreciably yet lacking feel. The car has a remarkable amount of lift-off and tuck-in which needed learning." Trailing throttle oversteer was also a problem because of the poor weight distribution.

Autocar did say that the car offered the driver a good seating position and had comfortable seats. However, anyone over six feet would find it

The 600 offered a more conventional dashboard with separate gauges and glovebox. Note how the shifter came through from the center of the dash.

If car design could be considered funky, the 1971 600 coupe easily qualifies. Styling is awkward and looks as though someone whittled down the original 600.

Rear view of the 600 coupe's "frogman" rear hatch. While the opening hatch aided access to the rear, space was still limited. The shape of the hatch also dictated luggage size. Road & Track

When a trunk was added to the 600 sedan, space was also at a premium. A conventional suitcase would never fit, and even groceries would be a squeeze. Soft goods are recommended.

cramped. Switches and controls were within easy reach and worked with precise action, and the testers loved the horn, describing it as a "light-hearted, cheerful beep."

The only comfort fault was in the heating. Imagine trying to get heat from the air-cooled, 599 cc motor. "Just when you want maximum warmth, it was not available," said *Autocar*.

On the whole, *Autocar* found the N600 enjoyable and a nice car for around town. Yet it also needed much development and redesign before it could seriously compete with the Mini or the Rootes Imp. In closing, the *Autocar* writer said, "It gave me a great deal of fun, despite its faults, never once let me down."

Shortly after this test came the N600G, essentially the same car as the N600 with only some cosmetic changes. The dash got some fake wood covering, and a console of sorts was put in to absorb the shift-lever vibration and rattles. An odd side note is that although this car offered a tachometer, the follow-up Civics did not get one until 1973.

A sporty three-spoke steering wheel with a smart leather wrap was substituted for the previous two-spoke plastic wheel. Final refinements included carpet and different door handles. The only mechanical change was the much-needed front disc brakes. This upscale model came at a premium of 90 pounds sterling. *Autocar* questioned its value.

Most surprising about the 600 was that while it looked like a hatchback, the entire rear did not open. There was merely a tiny opening compartment making a trunk of sorts. Despite this limiting factor, 3,770 units were sold in the United States that inaugural year.

In 1971, Honda gave us two models: the 600 two-door sedan and the 600 coupe. The drivetrain carried over from the previous year for both cars, but the coupe sported all-new sheet metal. The new coupe had the same running gear as the sedan; however, its new bodyshell was even more awkward and stubby than its predecessor. An opening rear hatch that resembled a diver's mask was added, making the car more practical, and the amount of storage space behind the back seat was surprising. Although Honda still offered the most basic creature comforts, sales jumped to nearly 10,000 units that year, and sales doubled to just over 20,000 cars for 1972, with the same two models offered again.

The cars were remarkably fun to drive, perhaps because they were so small. While the outer bodyshell appeared small, there was ample room in the passenger compartment for two and the small rear seat accommodated two adults for short distances. Traveling with any more than two people and their luggage presented problems as the cargo area was still limited.

The interior appointments were a stark mixture of vinyl, plastic and metal. The seats were shapeless and had absolutely no feel or support; it was rather like sitting on a springy church pew. There was plenty of travel for taller drivers, and the seats reclined all the way back, but having the seats at the end of the track eliminated any room for rear passengers. The rear seat also folded down to make more cargo space, and the full-size, ten-inch spare tucked under the rear deck. Rubber matting took the place of carpet, and the textureless interior panels rose halfway up to meet the finished interior of the body. One nice feature was a small overhead console in the coupe, housing a domelight and a swiveling map light.

Although there was not a lot of power, the cars moved along quite well. The ride was rather stiff and clunky and you felt every bump, but bodyroll was minimal even in a sharp corner. Corners could not be taken too sharply as the car had a turning circle of thirty-one feet, wide for a car this small. As a daily commuter the car was a dream: it offered high mileage and a 78 inch wheelbase that could be parked just about anywhere, maybe even the motorcycle spot.

If you run across one of these little gems, don't be surprised if your local Honda dealer refuses to work on it; few do.

First generation, 1973–79

The 1973 new model introductions in the fall of 1972 brought the first Honda Civic to the world. The car had grown a bit, gaining nearly eight inches in the wheelbase, and it was fitted with twelve-inch wheels. The body design was far less quirky, but its resemblance to the 600 series was obvious.

The most important difference was Honda's new four-cylinder, water-cooled engine. The 1200 cc engine delivered a modest 50 hp, but most importantly it was a smoother, bigger, more pleasant car to drive.

Again, the dashboard was rather featureless with only a small pod in front of the driver, but the gearshift lever had been moved to the floor. The car still had a manual choke mounted to the left of the wheel.

The 600's big brother, the Civic. Pictured is a 1975 Civic CVCC. Road & Track

Interior trim on the first-generation Civics was nearly as plain as its predecessors. This 1975 Civic illustrates the vinyl bench-like seats offering little support and vinyl door panels with metal trim. Note the plastic two-spoked steering wheel and simple dash display. The manual choke is located to the left of the wheel. Honda

Civic's first tachometer arrived in 1974, and the temperature and fuel gauges moved to a separate pod to the right of the main instrument pod. This model also had a sportier metal-spoked wheel. Road & Track

25

Along with the standard four-speed gearbox, Honda also offered a two-speed semi-automatic transmission known as the Hondamatic. The name alone may evoke memories of the Mini-matic transmission found in the English Minis, but Honda's was a far cry from the British version.

Honda realized that a major portion of the American market only drove cars with automatic transmissions and it was only offering cars with manual transmissions. About that time, Mazda, Toyota and Nissan had gotten together to form JAT, the Japanese Automatic Transmission company. The three were working to solve the same problem faced by Honda. JAT quickly came up with a fully automatic three-speed transmission for all their cars, which they also offered to Honda. However, the transmission was rejected by Honda because it was primarily used for rear-wheel-drive cars and they only had front-wheel drive.

Originally, Honda had experimented with a Borg-Warner automatic, but Honda's independent nature motivated the company to build its own. The Hondamatic was quite similar to Volkswagen's automatic stick shift. It was a torque converter unit with a floor-mounted lever that was placed in low to start and moved up to high range at about 20 mph. It worked quite well and was reliable, especially since you could rev it out in low to get speed up before shifting to high. Low was the equivalent of second gear, and high took you out to about fourth.

The interior was much improved over the 600 series. The seats had more contour, and texture was added to the vinyl. The dashboard featured a long shelflike expanse with an instrument pod rising up in front of the driver. The pod contained two circles divided by a strip of illuminating ideograms. The fuel and temperature gauges occupied the left circle with the speedometer in the right. The dashboard was accented with a strip of vinyl that was supposed to look like wood trim. It really looked out of place and was quickly cured because as the car aged it would curl and peel off. Honda dropped it a few years later.

Honda made only slight changes to the 1973 Civic for the 1974 model year. The notable, but hardly noticeable, changes were the addition of a seatbelt interlock system, which would not allow you to start the car unless the belt was fastened, and the addition of an air pump to meet federal emissions regulations. The car was thus dubbed the "Air Car," as they were noisier than the previous models, and the anti-afterburn valve would occasionally stick causing the car to backfire through the exhaust. These back raps posed no danger but did tend to blow open a muffler from time to time.

World events and some new models brought great prosperity to Honda in 1975. The United States was facing the fuel crunch of the Arab oil embargo, and gas prices were sky-rocketing. The federally mandated emissions systems had just about smothered all the power from US and imported car engines which were forced to use the higher-priced unleaded fuel. America was still building large, heavy cars with big motors and low mpg figures. "Economy Car" was a new term that US car builders were still learning, but they were able to deliver the Ford Pinto and Mercury Bobcat in 1971.

Honda introduced two new cars and a new engine in 1975. A four-door wagon was added to the existing two-door sedan and two-door hatchback models, plus a special new five-speed, two-door hatchback was offered. Most important was Honda's new CVCC four-cylinder engine.

CVCC is Honda's registered trademark for their advanced stratified charge engine. CVCC abbreviates Controlled Vortex Combustion Chamber. In simple terms, this engineering was the secret of the Honda en-

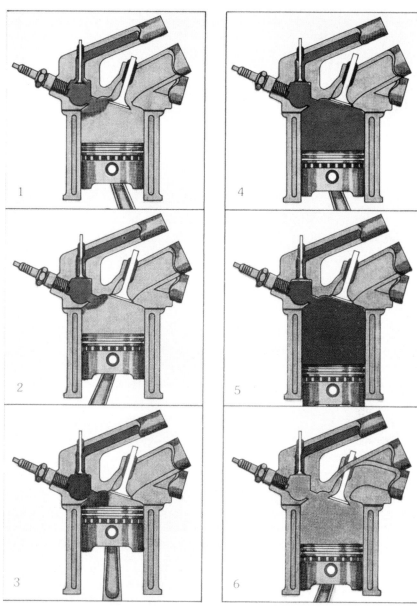

Honda's revolutionary CVCC power-plant. The design allowed the Civic to deliver optimum fuel economy, run on regular gas and meet emission standards with catalytic converters or air pumps.

gine's ability to run on regular fuel without being stifled by all the emission controls and to continue to deliver high gas mileage. An experiment was tried using the same engineering principles on a Chevy V-8 from the same era. It was able to run on regular fuel and delivered very high mileage. Why didn't everyone use this development to save us from the high fuel prices? Simple: no one was willing to pay Honda the royalties.

The little 1200 cc motor was able to deliver plenty of smooth revving power and render just over thirty miles per gallon—a big number in those days! The main selling feature was the car's ability to run on the less-expensive regular gas and still meet emissions requirements.

The wagon was simply an elongated hatchback with two more doors. Honda's efficient use of space made this a roomy car, able to hold quite a bit of cargo. The new five-speed hatchback was the notable model for 1975, Honda's first sporty car since the 600 coupe. Little was changed from the base hatchback, other than the obvious addition of another slot in the gearbox.

The five-speed gave the motor better range and dropped the cruising revs by about 500 rpm. There was also a slight upgrade to the interior with some different trim on the seats and door panels, plus the car featured the first tachometer offered since the 600 series. The new tachometer filled the left circle in the driver's pod, and the fuel and temperature gauges moved to the center of the "shelf." Honda's US sales had now jumped to over 102,000 units in just five short years, and it was about this time when Honda's carryover theme kicked in.

In 1975 only one option was added, the 1488 cc CVCC engine, a completely new powerplant. The reason for adding the larger engine was to make up for the power lost due to the CVCC configuration. The new larger engine had a power output of 53 hp while the 1200cc engine pumped out 52 hp.

In the mid-seventies, Honda also offered a number of accessories for the Civic, including a vinyl top, luggage rack, bodyside protective molding, rear defogger, hound's tooth patterned upholstery, armrests, cigarette lighter, console with false wood trim, wood or leather shift knob, FM radio and day/night mirror.

No additions or exceptions to the previous year's offerings were made in 1977. The larger engine and the new model had pushed sales to nearly a quarter-million cars. All 1977 and earlier Civics can easily be identified by the one element that changed in 1978: the bumpers.

Prior to 1978, the turn signals and reverse lights appeared almost as afterthoughts. The front signal lights were mounted on top of the bumper, while the reverse lights hung below the rear bumper. In 1978, these lamps were integrated into their respective bumpers. The only exception was that the wagon still had the reverse lamps affixed in the original fashion.

The year 1979 brought no changes to the Civics.

Second generation, 1980–83

Honda made some changes to the Civic for 1980, and important ones at that! The little car had accounted for nearly 300,000 units sold in 1979, and it finally grew up a bit as Honda debuted the second generation of Civics.

The cars offered a completely new look with a two-inch longer wheel-base and all-new skin. The new body design was an obvious evolution for the Civic. The lines from the first-generation cars were smoothed out and finished, and gone were the ties to the 600. The car also featured large rubber rub-strips on the doors and bumpers.

The beauty was more than skin deep. Under the squared-off new hood came your choice of a 1300 cc or 1500 cc CVCC engine, and a four- or five-speed gearbox was standard depending on which model you ordered.

The Civic only received minor revisions, such as trim items and new locations for parking lights and reverse lights. Nevertheless, the reverse lamps still appear bolted on as an afterthought. The Civic was completely re-modeled in 1981; here is a second-generation 1983 model. The connection to the first Civic is visible, yet the car was entirely different from the wheels up.

When the Civic was redesigned in 1981, it also sprouted two more doors. This became one of Honda's most popular designs, so popular that it forced Honda to phase out the upscale Civic hatchback coupe. Obviously a product of the square-style days.

One of Honda's most ingenious and convenient options was the rear wiper and washer introduced with the second-generation models.

29

Honda's new fully automatic three-speed transmission was an extra-cost option on all models. Wheels grew a bit as well with thirteen-inch rollers, and radial tires were standard on the 1500 while the 1300 kept the bias-ply twelve-inchers. The suspension was also improved with fully independent MacPherson struts at all the corners on all models, except for the wagon that retained the rigid axle and leaf springs.

The Civic family's metamorphosis resulted in several models being offered. The sedan was gone, and only the hatchbacks remained in 1300 and 1500 forms. In the two sizes, DX and GL models were offered. DX meant Deluxe, and in keeping with their value-for-the-dollar formula, the DX models came with more standard features and a few more niceties in the passenger compartment, while the hatchbacks had no frills and cost less. The GL models were top-of-the-line and packed with options and nicer trim.

Again, Honda was beating other car builders to the punch by offering packages rather than itemized options that carried individual price tags. Things like digital clocks, day/night mirrors, vanity mirrors, side-window defoggers, rear-window wipers and the like don't affect the performance of the car but do make the buyers feel as if they are getting more car for their coins. Honda offered coin boxes too. All these little amenities were able to woo the Americans into buying 500,000 Hondas.

The passenger compartment was also new: nicer seats, headliner, carpets and door panels—and a new dashboard. The seats offered a bit more lumbar support and nicer coverings with your choice of vinyl or cloth. Unfortunately, the Japanese car builders were doing everything right in the late seventies except for carpets. Whether it was a Mazda, Toyota, Honda or any of the others, the carpet came apart, curled up, tore or quickly wore out. They all seemed to remedy the problem by 1979 and 1980 models.

The new dashboard retained an element from the previous Civics. The pod and shelf were modernized with some new contours and softer plastic. The shelf was just a small ledge at the center of the dashboard; below it were the heater controls with the radio at the bottom. A larger glovebox was installed, and all electrical buttons and knobs were moved

Honda's second generation of Civics sported a molded-plastic dashboard, which was much more appealing than those on previous Civics. The most welcomed change was the absence of the *stick-on fake wood trim. All controls on the new display were easily within reach. The uninspiring two-spoked plastic wheel was retained.*

left of the steering wheel, with wipers on the right stalk and lights on the left. Oddly enough, the rear defogger and wiper switches were mounted on the side of the pod. New speaker enclosures were incorporated into the far ends of the fascia.

The instruments set deeper in the pod, and a variety of dials were offered depending on the model. The gauges themselves were also brought up to date in appearance with red needles and larger numerals. Following the trend of the day, the speedometer only went as far as 85 mph. The metal spokes in the steering wheel were replaced by two plastic spokes in the base models and four spokes in the DX cars.

Once again, Honda's simple but effective marketing was going strong. Buyers did little picking and choosing of colors, fabrics and options as they would have with American dealers. Instead, you bought a Honda because you liked a particular package, model or color. Moreover, probably the instrument cluster or the radio was the deciding factor. The

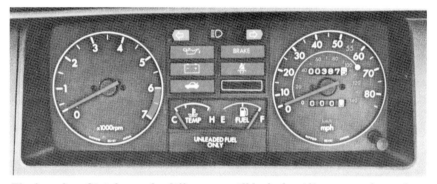

The four-door Civic boasted a different fascia, and it appeared as though Honda tried to make it something special as this was a new car. The dash still looked as if it were made up of several parts grouped together, and the radio was completely out of place. Honda

Flagship of the Civic line was the GL, later displaced by the four-door. This model featured the best of all Civic dashes to date. Note that both the four-door and GL feature a four-spoked steering wheel, which looked much better than the two-spoked version.

cars came in a trio or so of colors that were more conservative than the oranges and yellows of the 1970.

This second generation of Civics only endured through the 1983 model year. During that time little changed on any of the models, although Honda made several notable refinements.

In 1981, Honda debuted the four-door Civic. To accommodate the two new ports, the wheelbase was stretched from 88.6 to 91.3 inches which pushed the overall length twenty inches to 161. This was also the first Civic with a bona fide trunk!

The front end boasted a new grille and the square headlights that were so popular in America at the time. The four-door was the only car that featured the new cosmetics for 1981, but the entire cast of Civics received the same treatment in 1982. The new big sedan also had a slightly different dash display not used in any other models.

The 1980 and 1981 models have a problem with the vent system freezing in the colder climates. This is easily remedied by placing cardboard between the grille and the radiator. Do not block the entire radiator! Leave about a third of it clear to cool the motor. Honda does not recommend this fix because it won't tell you the vents freeze, but if you want warm toes, you had best cut up a box.

By 1983, Honda realized that people who wanted a luxury Civic would buy the four-door and not the GL, so the company dropped the GL from the line-up. In its place came the first truly sporty Civic, the S model. These were also the first Civics to come in colors other than the conservative "accountant" hues. You had only two options: red or black. Trim and bumpers were matte black on both cars, with a red-orange stripe on the side moldings and bumpers. This gave the red edition some nice accenting, while the black car had the European monochrome look.

The S models were only offered with the 1500 cc engine and a five-speed gearbox. The transmission was not the standard usually coupled with the bigger engine; rather, it came with the final drive ratio from the 1300! This odd couple under the hood gave the car a much shorter final drive ratio than the rest of the Civic family. The S model was able to wind

Honda offered a sportier Civic in 1983, the S model. The car came in either black or white and featured extra torsion bars, special wheels, front air dam, special seats and all the options available on a Civic except air conditioning.

up through the gears quicker and had a snappier feel. The car felt quickest when you were riding alone; once you added a couple of adults, it lost quite a bit of its zip.

The rest of the car received attention as well: fatter tires, accented wheels, firmer shocks, and front and rear anti-sway bars. The S and the rest of the Civic line fitted with the 1500 engine also received ventilated front disc brakes for the first time.

The exterior was not the only recipient of sporty upgrades. Inside you found a new steering wheel, black dashboard, nicer door panels with map pockets and new cloth seats. The seats in either color car were black with red inserts and heavy side bolsters. They were comfortable and held you firmly in place during spirited cornering. The car came fully loaded with intermittent wipers, rear defogger, and rear wiper and washer. The only options were air conditioning and a radio.

The S model was the only Civic of the second generation that could handle spirited cornering; the rest of the line-up severely lacked the performance aspects of driving fun. The heart of the problem was the suspension and tires in base Civics. Tossing any of the cars into a corner gave you the sensation that either it was going to tip over or the front tires were going to curl under the car. A meatier tire like the Michelin XVS fitted to the S could help out, but the big difference was the enhanced suspension. One drawback to the stiffer bars and shocks was a stiff ride, with every bump echoing in the passenger compartment with a thud.

Excluding the S models, the rest of the Civics were well-mannered road cars that delivered miles and miles of trouble-free, economical transportation. The little CVCC engines would purr so low at idle that you sometimes had to check to make sure yours was running, and they would rev strong all the way to redline.

The S was well-mannered too, but because of its gearing it was the first Honda to show notable torque-steer. Launching the car off the line would make the wheel tug strongly to the right, and keeping the revs in the power band on a rough road surface would give you quite a bit of bump-steer as well. The steering in the S model seemed to be a bit tighter and offer more feel than the others.

The S was the first Honda that you could really drive hard and it would stand up to it. The earlier Civics would tolerate mild abuse, but after they aged a bit, things began to break. How many times have you seen a pizza man driving through your neighborhood in an older Civic, with tires squealing and about to fold under the car, a hole in the muffler and rusty fenders, as he tries to make his deadline? The older cars could not take it; the S could.

You don't see many of the first series Civics around, especially if you live in the colder climates where salt is used on the roadways. The earliest ones simply dissolved, and no doubt the bodies gave way long before the drivetrains were ready to give up. The rear hatches and front fenders were most susceptible to the evils of rust, which spreads relentlessly. You can still find old Civics in the South and the West with oxidized blue, orange or yellow paint.

I rolled up 70,000 miles in my own black 1500S and enjoyed every minute of it. I even drove it through a few tough Minnesota winters, the paint held up beautifully and it had only the tiniest rust bubble on the tailgate when I sold it. I must confess that it was rustproofed and the plastic fender liners helped the longevity of the front clip.

I modified mine slightly by replacing the Honda carburetor with a Weber DGV. It bolted right on in an afternoon with the aid of an adaptor plate and a hex wrench. It did increase power, but I don't know that it was the thirteen percent increase advertised. I was able to beat just about any other similar displacement car that challenged me. It also gave a much throatier tone as the two big barrels groped for air. One drawback is that the aluminum adaptor plates can crack from heat after 30,000 miles, but they are easily replaced.

The end of 1983 put Honda's total US sales over 400,000 units, a fast and dramatic climb.

Third generation, 1984–87

In 1984, we come to the third generation of Civics and the birth of the CRX. All the CRX's kin, the new Civic models, received dramatically reworked sheet metal, new engines and new suspension, but all still resembled the CRX in the hood and grille.

The 1987 Civic four-door could only be described as boxy. It appeared to be a smaller version of the second-generation cars.

Dashboards in the third-generation Civic moved toward a flat look with a small shelf reminiscent of the first series. Controls and the radio were all in the same line. Although still plastic, this 1987 model offered a much nicer steering wheel. Honda

The third-generation wagons fell into the awkward styling category. Outward visibility was excellent, and these were the first four-wheel-drive Hondas.

34

The new hatchback was simply a CRX with an elongated roofline and vertical rear door. The base hatchback came with only one trim option and a four-speed stick while the DX came with a five-speed or the Hondamatic. Winner of the most substantial change was the wagon, looking much like an oversized Honda City. The roofline was tall compared to the slanting hood, and the window treatment in the cargo area was unique. The four-door sedan kept the CRX nose but had a high roofline and a squared-off rear end. The Civic was nearly a four-seat CRX, and an Si model was added in 1986 with the same fuel-injected engine as in the two-seat model. Much to the dismay of many CRX owners, the car had virtually the same performance characteristics.

All models shared the same running gear and interior appointments. The only exception was the different wagon with its own dashboard and seats. The cars remained virtually the same, with only a few changes, through 1987.

In 1985 the first Honda four-wheel-drive wagon was introduced. The extra drive wheels were engaged manually and essentially gave the car a six-speed gearbox by adding an ultra-low first gear. In 1987 the system was upgraded with a fluid coupling that engaged the additional drive wheels automatically when needed. This system was called Real Time 4WD.

Honda had significant changes on the burner but only made simple changes in 1986. The fuel-injected engines were now offered in the entire Civic line-up. Everything remained status quo for 1987.

Fourth generation, 1988

In 1988, the fourth generation of the Civic appeared. Again, all-new skin covered Honda's latest refinements. There were quite a few refinements: the entire line got new 1488 cc fuel-injected engines and the new double wishbone suspension.

The new styling showed a logical evolution from the cars of 1987. The lines were smoother, rounder and more aerodynamic—easily the best-looking of recent Civics. The lines on the four-door sedan have been carried out to where I think they should have been when the car was restyled

The restyled 1988 Civic benefited greatly from the new double-wishbone suspension. The result was a lower, cleaner design with smooth lines and plenty of interior room. Compare this four-door to the previous version. Honda

The body panels on the 1988 Civic hatchback were also completely redone, thanks to the new suspension. While it resembled its predecessor, it had a more raked windshield and smoother lines.

35

The 1988 wagon is another example of how the fourth-generation Civic benefited from the new suspension platform: smoother, cleaner lines. The four-wheel-drive was updated in 1988 with the additional driving wheels activated as needed.

A rear spoiler of sorts was added to the 1988 models to help channel air away from the rear window and keep dirt from clinging.

A rare site on American streets: the 1987 Honda City Turbo.

Modular is the best way to describe the fourth edition of the Civic's display. Instruments and controls flow together nicely; however, heater controls and the radio appear added on, and gauges look to be in a separate pod. Note the upgraded seat bolsters and matching trim inserts in the door panels. The steering wheel is nicer for 1988. Honda

in 1984. This 1988 sedan is one of the sexiest-looking Civics since their inception. Speaking of better looks, the wagon has been reshaped for 1988 with smoother, less staccato lines. It is the best-looking wagon since the introduction of the second series back in 1980.

Although the Civic still derived from the CRX, the two nameplates went their separate ways: the Civic badge was dropped from the CRXs.

Driving

First, I have to say that the 1988 models are better; in fact, the 1988 models are an absolute joy to drive. They are smooth, quiet and have ample power to get you around town. They don't snap to redline like the CRX, but they weren't made to. They live up to Honda's theme of economical family-oriented cars.

Life with a Civic is simple because the car is simple. All the models from the first series are well-mannered road cars that will run forever if you just remember to follow the maintenance chart. Oil is important. Use 5W-30 in colder climates and 10W-30 where it gets hot, and change it often. It is quite easy to do minor servicing at home since everything is easy to reach and parts are plentiful.

Out on the open road, the little CVCC engine purrs without missing a beat, and you rarely have to think about getting gas. All pre-1980 CVCCs take regular gas, and that stuff is getting a little harder to find but is not nearly as scarce as high-octane pure premium. If necessary, the car will burn unleaded as well.

Some models are a bit noisy. There is not a lot of insulation, so road hum is fairly evident but not obtrusive. Seats are comfortable enough for the long hauls, but they could use more thigh support. Most have minimal or no side bolsters at all, so you will have to use alternate methods to stay in your seat during fast corners.

Cornering and road handling are not the Civic's strong suit, but the newest models perform much better than the older cars. There is a great deal of bodyroll in all of them, and it's hard to avoid feeling like the wheels are going to fold under the car. Much of this can be remedied with a better tire and some suspension modifications.

A race-prepped 1970 300 at Japan's Suzuka racetrack. Note the front spoiler and rear wing. Christopher Wallwork

The first racing Civic in America, King Motorsports' 1975 Civic.

Chapter 3

CRX

The $10,000 Porsche

It has been called the Mini Cooper of the 1980s, Boy Racer, Rollerskate GT, Pocket Rocket, Baby Bullet, Egg and even the $10,000 Porsche. It has also been named *Motor Trend's* Import Car of the Year—twice! These are not meant to be aliases because it is no secret that the Honda CRX and the CRX Si are snappy little sports cars that turn heads as well as tires. Whichever moniker you like, there is no denying that the car is quick, economical and lots of fun.

The CRX does indeed live up to all its nicknames. The Si is a giant-killer in the same sense that the Mini Cooper S teased the big boys during the sixties, and if offers nearly all the comforts and performance of many pricey European imports. A friend takes particular exception to this because my Si can run equal 0–60 mph and quarter-mile times with his 944. That's not to say the Porsche is a slug; rather, the Honda is a match for one of the world's highly regarded marques.

Since its debut, the Si has raced to the top of the CRX trio and continued to be Honda's most talked-about car. This is not surprising as the history of the trio is a story of innovation.

Honda's revolutionary CRX debuted in Japan in 1983 and in the United States in 1984. The car featured plastic lower body panels and plastic front fenders. Lower panels were always gray, while the upper body came in white, red or blue. The CRX also came with a black rear spoiler and stamped steel wheels.

The first CRX, 1983

The CRX was introduced to the United States in 1984 but originally debuted in Japan in 1983. Japan's version was a 1.5 liter four-cylinder that looked every bit like the American model. The cast-aluminum, overhead-cam engine pumped out 100 hp at 6000 rpm. That's pretty respectable when you consider the entire powerplant only weighed 203 lb.

Japan's first CRX was hotter than the American version. For openers, the Far Eastern version cranked out thirty-four more horsepower thanks to electronic port fuel injection. The first US model was supplied by a three-barrel Keihin carburetor. Cosmetically, the Japanese version had flip-up eyebrows above the rectangular headlights and the electric up-and-out sunroof that did not come across the Pacific Ocean until the 1985 Si.

In either US or Japanese trim, the CRX was a revolutionary design featuring a blend of modern materials, excellent fuel economy and good performance at a low, perhaps even steal of a, price.

This offering should not have surprised anyone when you consider an engineering-driven company like Honda. The lightweight construction and plastic body panels were truly state-of-the-art, and the new design was completely removed from any of its predecessors. Honda designs cars differently from the rest of the mass producers; it works alone where design and marketing are concerned, and strives to create cars that are targeted to their market. No clone cars allowed.

The CRX originated from Honda's M/M concept: maximum interior space, minimum exterior space. All Civics for the 1984 model year were developed using this new design theory, and they shared many elements including suspensions, engines and transaxles. The similarities ended there.

The first American 1.3 liter CRX HF and 1.5 liter base model were virtually identical in appearance, yet minor tuning changes under the hood accounted for big changes on the road. The same basic engine design has carried through all four years of the CRX with only minor changes.

The engine featured a cast-aluminum block and cast-aluminum cross-flow head with two valves per cylinder. The 1.5 version featured three valves; two smaller valves delivered the fuel mixture and one larger valve sent the exhaust air on its way.

The HF designation was added to the 1.3 liter version in 1985. This stood for High Fuel economy, and fuel consumption was 51 mpg in the city, 67 mpg on the highway. It was still the 1342cc aluminum engine but with some ingenious fuel-saving techniques. The HF featured two valves and utilized the CVCC pre-chamber system. The combustion chamber was a slightly advanced version of the CVCC system that is synonymous with the Civic. The system consisted of two chambers, one burning a rich mixture and the other a lean mixture for a hotter, more efficient bang. Honda was able to cut engine friction by five to ten percent by dropping a piston ring leaving two and by boosting compression to 10:1 while the faster 1.5 was at 9.2:1.

More fuel was saved by having the throttle closed during deceleration, and the alternator only charged the battery during deceleration to reduce drag on the engine. Honda even went as far as changing the alternator's output between acceleration and deceleration to cut drag. The camshaft was hollow to save weight, valve lift was reduced and the 1.3 had softer valve springs. Gas was delivered through a three-barrel Keihin carburetor.

All said and done, the HF version tipped the scales some eighty pounds lighter than its larger displacement brother and 700 pounds less than the Pontiac Fiero.

You no doubt believe that all these miserly methods gave the 1.3 HF the performance of a Chevette diesel with an automatic. Hardly! Granted it was not a screamer, but the 1342 cc motor produced 60 hp at 5500 rpm, which was ample power for the lightweight frame.

Gearboxes made the difference. The faster model came with a five-speed, while the 1.3 came with only four. The 1.3 had a much taller ratio, and the rpm fell much farther between shifts. Axle ratio was also different: 3.58:1 in the 1.3 and 4.27:1 in the 1.5. This simply meant that fuel was saved by keeping the engine from spinning any more than necessary.

Just to make sure you didn't use any fuel unnecessarily, Honda put an upshift light in the dash. The 1.3 also came with fewer frills; it lacked a digital clock, passenger-side mirror and other niceties.

Honda took that same engine and carburetor and lengthened the stroke from 78 mm to 86.5 mm to produce the 1.5 liter 1488 cc performance version. Obviously, the largest difference was in the head with a three-valve unit in this model. This cranked horsepower up to 76 hp at 6000 rpm and still kept fuel economy at 35 mpg. Performance-hungry Honda fans were already dreaming of the fuel-injected version that was available in Europe at the same time.

The 1.5 liter version was a pretty strong performer and zipped from 0–60 mph in just a tick over ten seconds. The European model turned in a time just under nine seconds. You can see the difference fuel injection made.

The 1.5 version's quickness placed it far ahead of its 1984 contemporaries like the Fiero, EXP and Pulsar NX, and put it in the middle of the pack of some tougher sports cars including the Mazda RX-7, Toyota Celica GT-S and VW GTI. The CRX's quickness sprang from the M/M concept, which could also be construed as Minimal Mass; the CRX in hot trim weighed just 1,800 lb., and the miserly model tipped the scales at 1,720. This incredibly light frame coupled with the 76 hp engine figured out to be a little more than twenty-five pounds per horsepower. That was respectable when you compared it to many other sports cars.

The first CRXs came with minimal transmission—actually transaxle—options. The 1.3 hatchback received only a four-speed, while the 1.5 arrived with a five-speed or the optional three-speed automatic.

The chassis also changed dramatically. The old Civic-style front coil springs were replaced by torsion bars to lower the hoodline and allow more space in the engine bay. And just after we grew accustomed to the independent rear suspension, Honda went back to a solid-beam rear axle. This move was designed to improve handling under all kinds of loads and make more room in the rear for such loads. Both models had front anti-roll bars.

Both models also offered rack-and-pinion steering, but the 1.3 got a quicker ratio than the 1.5. The reasons for the difference were twofold. First, the 1.3 had smaller tires which required the quicker ratio to bring it up to par. Second, the rear anti-roll bar in the 1.5 quickened steering response; Honda felt that putting the 1.3 liter's steering in the 1.5 would be too fast for some drivers. I can't say that there was a noticeable difference—both were light and nimble, perhaps a bit too light for performance-minded drivers who were accustomed to a heavier and slower steering setup. Even at rest there was little resistance in the wheel, and at speed you could turn either model with only a finger or two.

On the outside of all these engineering marvels was a tight little bodyshell made of steel and plastic. Everything below the rub-strips and bumpers was plastic including the bumpers themselves, molded into the front fenders. It was fairly easy to identify the plastic panels on the first series of CRXs because no matter what color the car was, the lower panels were dark gray. The fenders, however, were red, blue or white, the colors offered in 1984.

Plastic was no stranger to us in 1984 since we had heard so much about the new Pontiac Fiero made entirely of plastic. One of the Fiero's big selling points was that the holes for the body panels were drilled on the assembly line so everything fit tight. Honda only used plastic where the company determined it was necessary, and the tolerances were so close that you never had to worry about gaps between body panels. Honda's advertising campaign for the CRX's debut stressed the use of plastic and the body's resistance to rust. I haven't seen a rusty CRX yet, have you?

Little on the outside of the cars differentiated the two models. In fact, the marking on a car, other than the chrome Honda badges, was limited to a small 1.5 or HF insignia under the right taillamp. The 1.5 also came with a chrome-tipped exhaust pipe and a small, black spoiler-like wing mounted on the rear deck, while the 1.3 had neither.

The 1984 through 1986 CRXs featured recessed, square headlamps. The European version had small headlamp doors that rose when the lights were on.

Rear view of the 1984 CRX. Note the single chrome exhaust pipe exiting on the right side of the car. This also offers a good look at the rear spoiler. The spoiler could break easily if it were used as a pushing point when the car was stuck. Also visible are the rear louvers, which could be purchased from Honda or aftermarket dealers.

41

The best part of all this advanced engineering, fuel economy and fun was the price tag: only $6,000 for the HF and $500 more for the quicker 1.5.

Birth of the CRX Si, 1985

The CRX's second birthday passed with no remarkable or even interesting changes in either version. In mid-1985, however, Honda gave us the CRX we had been dreaming of. The CRX Si was born from the 1.5 coupe, with the simple addition of fuel injection. No, it was not a Bosch Jetronic system or even a Zenith system. Naturally it was Honda's own.

As explained earlier, Honda doesn't share. If it experimented and came up with its own automatic transmission, why couldn't Honda make its own fuel injection? The Honda system was an electronic, computer-controlled sequential-port system that monitored exhaust temperature, crankshaft speed and position, air intake velocity, throttle position and coolant temperature to deliver the correct amount of fuel at precisely the right moment. The addition of fuel injection boosted horsepower from 76 to 91 hp, and torque jumped from 84 to 93 lb-ft.

The only other physical changes were at the roof and wheels of the car. The Si got an electric sunroof and alloy wheels that were half-an-inch wider than the stamped steel wheels on the 1.5. Tires remained Michelin MXLs on all models. The car still featured the beam axle with trailing links, and a sway torsion bar was mounted inside the rear axle on the CRX and Si models, but not in the HF.

The twenty percent increase in horsepower put the Si in a whole new performance league. The 60 mph mark came up on the clock in just under nine seconds, making the CRX Si a contender among the highly touted Omni GLH and VW GTI crowd—and meant even more fun for CRX drivers. The five-speed from the 1.5 was the only gearbox available for the Si.

It was the CRX Americans had been reading about. Or was it? The European and Asian models which had received the PGM FI (Pro-

In 1985 Honda introduced an Si version of the CRX. This model featured fuel injection, electric sunroof, aluminum wheels, dual chrome-tipped exhaust pipes and a slightly different rear spoiler. Other standard features included a rear wiper, defogger, and upgraded door and seat trim.

Close-up of the 1985 Si spoiler with rear wiper removed. This was also a tacked-on trim accessory, but was sturdier than the standard spoiler.

grammed Fuel Injection) one year earlier had on output of 100 hp and eight seconds separated the car from rest and 60 mph.

The interior of the Si was similar to the CRX, except that the rear deck spoiler was not a fin mounted to the rear vertical portion of the hatch. The Si also received dual chrome-tipped exhaust pipes, and black was added to the color options.

Second generation, 1986–87

By 1986, the rest of the United States knew how much fun CRX owners were having. US sales jumped from 500,000 in its introductory year to 640,000 just two years later. Naturally, while the US market was giggling and gloating over the new Si model, Europe and Asia had moved one up.

In the spring of 1985, Honda introduced a 1.6 liter, sixteen-valve, double-overhead-cam engine. That's right, a twin-cam with four valves per cylinder and 135 hp. Obviously, it was no easy task to bring this off. When you popped the little hood, you saw that the engine and all its plumbing went wall to wall.

The 1.6 dohc was the true giant-killer. A standing quarter-mile could be covered in sixteen seconds flat with a top speed of 86.5 mph; 60 mph was reeled off in just 7.5 seconds. That's enough to power past a Porsche 944 and an IROC Camaro.

In a 1985 road test, *Road & Track* said, "This performance came as a surprise to most of us, because the 16-valve engine does feel as though it is working hard when it is going quickly." Torque-steer was quelled with

In 1987, Honda restyled the front end on all CRXs with flush-mounted headlamps and offered a new Si. These odd-shaped lights were only available from Honda dealers. The Si had matching upper and lower body panels, new rear spoiler and new aluminum wheels; other CRX models still had gray lower panels. Pictured is a 1987 with a nose protector. Notice this protector does not shield the lights from debris. A replacement lens cost more than $100.

43

the use of a center-bearing support on the unequal length driveshafts. Honda made no other changes to the car, with the exception of a dohc decal below the bodyside molding at the rear of the doors and a folding jump seat in the rear, hardly big enough for children.

Meanwhile, back in the US market Honda changed the CRX Si for the new model year. Actually, refined is a better word.

Styling cosmetics were the most obvious change. The upper and lower body and bumpers all came in the same color, the nose and tail were redesigned and a few changes appeared on the inside.

The twelve-valve, fuel-injected engine remained at 91 hp, but the car gained a few pounds pushing the weight to a whopping 1,995 lb.

The most important engineering change occurred where the car met the road. The new Si was the first Honda to come with fourteen-inch wheels, and the old Michelin MXLs were replaced by fatter Yokohama AX 323s. This tire change gave the Si better grip in hard corners, but surprisingly, braking distances remained the same. The minimum stopping distance rivaled that of many cars equipped with anti-lock systems, but the tires left a bit to be desired.

I found the tires to be adequate on dry roads; however, they were poor in the wet and nearly worthless on the snow. It was unfortunate because if you were not getting good rubber on the road, all this performance was wasted. The base CRX retained the thirteen-inch wheels and 175/70 Michelin tires, and the HF kept the skinnier 165/70 Michelins.

Cosmetically, the changes were minor, but improved the look of the car greatly. The front end got some funky-shaped flush-mount headlamps, and the Si got some new grille work. On the tail end of the Si,

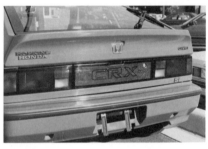

The rear spoiler on the 1987 Si was tucked on to the rear of the hatch rather than just below the window. It was made of soft urethane, while previous spoilers were hard plastic.

The flush side-mounted door handles of the 1987 CRX were a bit flimsy. These were changed to conventional handles in 1988.

44

the solid fin was removed and a more flowing spoiler was affixed to the hatch. The new fin was attached to a small panel that ran all the way across the rear. It was made of a soft polyurethane to resist breaking and denting. Honda is not one to buck a trend so the hip new ground effects were added to the Si models. These consisted of protruding side skirts just below the door sills and slight flares ahead of the rear wheels. The lower rear valance panel also extended straight down rather than tucking under the body as on the standard CRX.

The new body required special consideration. First, the curb-hunting front air dam was merely plastic bolted to plastic, and was easily damaged by steep driveways and curbs. Next, there were the new aerodynamic side moldings. The flares ahead of the rear wheels were easy targets for rocks and other road debris from the front wheels. While they did not look sporty, mudflaps prevented most of the damage. Last and most costly were the new headlight lenses. Breaking one will set you back about $110 per lens.

In 1988, Honda introduced an all-new CRX with completely revised body panels and interior. The lower, sleeker shape was derived from the use of double-wishbone suspension. The gray lower panels were eliminated, and a black non-chip plastic piece surrounded the lower skirt of the car. Shown is a 1988 HF. Honda

The 1987 and 1988 CRX Sis nose to nose illustrate the differences in design. All 1984 through 1988 CRXs featured the same chassis and skin. The newer model at the right had a lower hood line, more raked windshield and roof and completely restyled rear end.

In 1987, everything stayed nearly the same for the first time in CRX history. The most notable change was that the HF got the same 1488 cc engine as its bigger brothers. It remained an eight-valve, carbureted CVCC motor and still delivered an amazing 52 mpg in the city and 67 on the open roads. The only other change was the addition of silver as a color option for all models.

After carefully watching the evolution of the CRX, I purchased a 1987 model Si. I loved the way they looked and figured Honda was going to make some big changes in the CRX for 1988, especially with all the talk of a mid-engined model in the works. Well, it did make some big changes, not only to the CRX but also to the entire line-up.

Third generation, 1988

Honda made major changes to the CRX inside, outside and underneath. Let's start with what the cars have in common and then work our way up from the basic HF model to the *piece de resistance*, the Si. The trio's wheelbase grew four inches for 1988, and the wheels got new double wishbone suspension at both ends. Honda removed the MacPherson struts in the front and the rigid axle and trailing arms in the rear, but the back end kept the coil springs and tube shocks. These refinements gave the car a better ride and much improved handling, plus the compact design allowed for a lower hoodline.

Under the new hood were all sorts of new goodies. Both the HF and base CRX shared a new 1493 cc sequential-port, fuel-injected engine, but the base CRX got a sixteen-valve head while the HF retained the eight-

The European version of the 1988 CRX Si. It looked identical to the US version with the exception of the small bump on the hood, which made room for the twin-cam powerplant and its larger cam gears. Other amenities included four-wheel disc brakes, electric windows and mirrors, tilt steering wheel and what Honda termed an emergency rear seat. This was a small jump seat for children or adults for a short ride.

valve CVCC design. The latter was rated at 62 hp at 4500 rpm and 90 lb-ft of torque at 2000 rpm and still came in at 50 mpg in the city and 56 mpg on the highway. The additional valves in the CRX punched horsepower up to 92 at 6000 rpm but only 89 lb-ft of torque at 4500 rpm. The HF weighed in at 1,819 lb., while the base model tipped the scale at 1,922 lb. Here an interesting trend appeared. As the Si got bigger and better, the other two keep moving up to take its former place. Notice how the base CRX had all the specifications of the previous year's Si.

The Si got a completely new 1590 cc sixteen-valve powerplant that unleashed 105 horses at 6000 rpm and 98 lb-ft of torque at 5000 rpm. Unlike the competition, the sixteen little valves operated off just one hollow camshaft to save weight and expense. The new Si also broke the one-ton barrier by seventeen pounds, but the increase in power made up for the increased mass.

At last, the ultimate in sophisticated engineering? Not quite. Once again the cars across the ocean got a few extra goodies that might be worth waiting for on US shores. The Euro version looked virtually identical to the US one, with the exception of the steering wheel on the right side in the United Kingdom and a small bump on the hood. That bump made room for the double-overhead-cam, sixteen-valve engine that pumped out 123 hp at 6700 rpm. The red band came up at 7250 rpm.

If that was not enough to make your blood hot, the Euro version also received power-assisted four-wheel disc brakes and a host of comfort goodies we could only wish for, like the small folding jump seat, power windows and power mirrors. The windows and mirrors were nice extras, but imagine how much fun the going and stopping power was! Adding to the fun was a different muffler system with a tougher sports car note.

Unfortunately, it does not look as though the US market will ever get this version of the twin-cam, sixteen-valve engine; however, we will be getting the same four-wheel disc brakes soon, according to a Honda official. (Those of you who cannot wait for the twin-cam, mega-valve power under the hood of your CRX may find it interesting that the twin-cam 113

A 1987 twelve-valve, left, versus the 1988 sixteen-valve, right. Notice the close proximity of the newer model's engine to the hood versus that of the older model. The drawback to this low clearance was that bugs would actually bake onto the paint because the engine was so close to the hood.

The clean appearance of the 1988 sixteen-valve CRX motor.

hp Integra engine will fit in the CRX. It is a tight fit, but even the motor mounts match up.)

Both the 1988 Euro and US models got all-new skin from front to rear. The lower body side and front clip were still plastic, but Honda did away with the gray two-tone treatment. Instead, the cars came in solid colors, including the bumpers, but all had black rocker panels below the doors. The panels deflected road debris, preventing unsightly stone scars.

The windshield was raked more than on the previous CRXs, the rear wing had vanished even on the Si and all the cars returned to more conventional door handles rather than the sideways, flush-mounted style. The cars also got some new window treatment with longer rear-quarter windows and a funky, shaded glass panel in the back for better rear vision. One of Honda's best design efforts was the cargo bay. It provided much more security than in the previous models, and the ingenious locking storage area could be removed for hauling larger parcels.

The CRX's new fascia was Honda's first aesthetically pleasing dash design. All previous Civics and CRXs had somewhat choppy creations made up of individual sections without any continuity. The new model featured a smooth and flowing design as the edges of the instrument pod wound down into a center console. The center panel was slightly canted toward the driver, and all the controls were within fingertip reach unlike in previous models where you had to lean forward from either seat to get to the radio.

When I saw the 1988 CRX, I was glad I bought when I did because I didn't like the redesign, yet I was envious of the new interior appointments and technical advancements. It took some time for the aesthetics of the new body to grow on me, but today I think it was a logical step forward for the CRX, although I feel the rear end stops a bit too abruptly.

One of the most subtle changes for 1988 was dropping the designation Civic from the nameplate. The cars were Civic CRXs, but by 1988 the CRX stood alone as a separate model.

The restyled rear end of the 1988 CRX had a higher tail with a lip built into the design so there was no need for a spoiler.

The 1988 CRX Si wide open. This was the first CRX to have window frames. Windows in previous CRXs occasionally leaked water into the car from the weatherstripping. Notice the insulation under the hood; 1988 CRXs needed this because the engine was so close to the sloping hood.

Honda offered a variety of wheels on the CRX, but only a handful were truly appealing. This is the original 1984 wheel, which was stamped steel.

In 1985, a plastic gray lugnut cover was offered.

A smaller plastic hubcap was offered for 1986–1987 steel wheels.

An all-new steel wheel premiered in 1988.

The CRX Si naturally received the best wheels in the lineup. Here is the four-slot aluminum-alloy wheel that was standard in 1985.

The 1987 Si aluminum-alloy wheel with four telephone-dial holes.

The high-tech 1988 Si aluminum-alloy wheel, similar to the Integra's alloy wheel.

Ergonomics
Interior space

True to the M/M concept of design in the CRX, Honda provided maximum interior space. We found tons of legroom, ample headroom and plenty of cargo capacity for two people and all their travel necessities. Honda has been known for its little extra conveniences, ever since the coin boxes in the 1976 Accords. The CRX was no different, offering the coin box as well as a glovebox, a handy little closing compartment on the top of the dashboard and a small locking compartment in the rear. The Si models also featured map and door pockets plus a console cubby with slots for cassette tapes or the like.

The compartment on the dashboard was handy for storing your checkbook and sunglasses. The only problem was the hard plastic inside; anything heavy or metallic rattled around over bumps and in corners. Lining it with a swatch of felt or cloth hushed even a janitor's set of keys. It was easy to do as the entire assembly popped out after removing the Phillips screws.

At first glance, the large handle on the rear cubby looked like the ticket to a folding backseat, but it was simply a 23 by 12 by 3¼ inch lockable storage. It was nice for small items that you wanted to keep out of sight, but it was hardly Fort Knox. The lid was merely tagboard and any would-be thief would not have found it much of a hindrance.

The additional pockets offered in the Si added to the convenience, and the tape holder ahead of the shifter gave you deejay-like access to your favorite tunes.

The console cubby was standard on the Si, but you could purchase a similar one from your Honda parts counter. Anyone knowing the basics of screwdriver operation could pop in one in under an hour.

The rear hatch opened wide and high to access the twenty-plus cubic feet of cargo space. There was plenty of room for just about anything; however, the rear window had a steep slant so items as large as console TVs were a little tough to transport. Little of the rear panel goes up with the hatch which meant a considerable lift up and over the tail. The win-

Door panels in the pre-1984 CRXs were simple vinyl with some padding beneath. Two nice features included carpeted door-kick protection and built-in speaker compartments.

By 1987, the interior trim had improved with map pockets, door pulls and cloth inserts that matched the interior trim.

The restyling in 1988 brought about a whole new look. The lower portion was hard plastic with a large, perforated, far-from-subtle speaker enclosure, while the upper portion was padded vinyl with a cloth insert sporting the letters CRX. The kick protector was gone.

dow did leave cargo exposed, a situation Honda's cargo cover could remedy. You can pick one up at any dealer's parts counter for about $20. The other option is tinting the windows or adding louvers to the rear glass. Smoked glass is quite popular and does not look out of place on a CRX since most of the trim is black anyway. I do think that louvers look out of place on a CRX and give the car a humpback appearance.

Obviously, Honda gave serious consideration to space needs. If you were the kind of person with lots of stuff, there was a place to keep it in your CRX. One benefit Honda overlooked was cargo straps to secure smaller packages. You have undoubtedly shared my frustration with

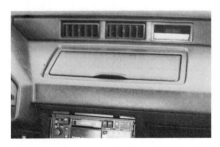

The CRX is naturally chock-full of all those little conveniences Honda adds to its cars. This flip-open compartment on the dash allows handy storage for sunglasses and the like. Hard objects tend to be noisy on the hard plastic interior, and it is advisable to pad the inside of the compartment with felt or cloth.

Nearly every pre-1988 CRX owner has been asked if there is a seat below that handle behind the seats. The locking storage provides a handy spot for medium-sized valuables. A full rear cargo cover is available from Honda dealers, although it is expensive.

The 1988 CRX featured a trunk within a hatchback. There is a storage ledge behind the seats with a compartment similar to that in previous CRXs plus a huge locking compartment that could be removed. Access was easy from the front seats or from the rear hatch.

The rear hatch on the 1988 CRX had a smoked glass panel for greater rearward visibility. The panel was difficult to see through from the outside, but it was easy to see through from within and dramatically enhanced the driver's vision. Had Honda not installed the rear panel, the driver would have had minimal rear vision.

The dash display on the first CRX was simple and driver oriented. Large gauges were easy to read and heater, wiper and light controls were at the fingertips. The only element out of reach was the radio. It was located at the lower center of the dash and the driver had to lean forward to operate it. The shifter console was not connected to the dash. The three-spoked steering wheel fitted to the 1984–1987 CRXs was unfortunately plastic and unbecoming to the sportiness of the car.

The only change that came in 1987 was a revision in the lower portion of the dash, which connected the floor console with the dash. This provided a handy cubby for storage of small items, and it had small partitions at the top to store cassette tapes. The three-spoked plastic steering wheel was hardly attractive or sporty.

The new skin in 1988 also brought a new dashboard, the best offered in a CRX. This was designed totally for the driver with a center console canted toward the pilot's seat and all controls at the fingertips. The new gauge layout was also appealing. Honda updated the three-spoked steering wheel; alas it was still plastic and uncomplementary to the sports car appeal of the CRX.

boxes, briefcases and the like sliding and banging around in the back. I've looked into rigging some straps, but there was no solid place to anchor the screws in all the plastic.

There is lots of plastic in the car, but what doesn't have lots of plastic these days? The difference was that Honda did it attractively. Everything was put together with top-quality fit and finish, and all the colors matched unlike in many domestic cars.

Instrumentation

Surprisingly, with all the changes in the CRX, we have only seen two different fascia arrangements. The 1988 edition marked the new and best design where ergonomics were concerned. Nothing was really wrong with the first design; the second was just that much better.

The earlier dash was attractive and put everything within fairly easy reach of the driver and passenger. The driver got a pod with a large, easy-to-read tachometer and speedometer divided by the usual column of warning lights. The fuel and temperature gauges occupied opposite lower corners. The one drawback to this layout was that with your hands in the optimal ten and two o'clock positions on the wheel, the two smaller needles were hard to see. Of course, we are talking CRX here, and how urgent was it that you keep tabs on fuel consumption?

Below the dials to the right were the delightful heater and vent controls. Soft-touch buttons allowed you to blow hot or cool air on the windshield, your feet or your face. These pneumatic switches first appeared in the Prelude in 1983 and were adapted to the rest of the line the following year. Three-speed fans originally came in the CRX, and a fourth setting was added in 1986.

The temperature controls took a bit of practice to get the desired comfort level. Those of us in colder climates discovered you could heat up the interior after going just a few blocks and melt the thickest ice off the front and side windows in no time. Unfortunately, all the heat radiated

Honda's push-button heater controls in the pre-1988 CRXs were effortless and could be activated without taking a hand from the wheel. The right spoke blocked part of the view, but once familiar a driver could tap them without looking.

The heater and fan controls were moved to the center console in the 1988 models. The driver's hand had to come off the wheel to operate them, but they were readily visible and within easy reach.

from behind the center of the dash, and you ended up with your right foot on fire and your other foot chilly. There was no real remedy short of tucking both feet toward the center of the dash.

If hot weather was your plight, the optional air-conditioning worked well with surprisingly little drain on the motor. At rest, however, the idle tended to dip down and the car shuddered a bit.

The other controls critical to operating the CRX were on the stalks left and right of the wheel. Lights, dimmer and directionals were to the left and wipers to the right. The wipers were one of Honda's nice standard features offering low and high speed plus a one-speed intermittent setting. A mist setting was added in 1985. The Si came standard with a rear wiper and washer controlled from the same stalk.

The only real problem with the first dash design was the placement of the radio. While it looked good where it was, neither passenger nor driver could reach it easily. When the seats were in comfortable cruising position, you had to lean forward to change stations or operate the tape player. The 1988 design put the bebop controls at your fingertips.

Put simply, the 1988 fascia design was superior. The entire layout was rethought and rebuilt for optimum driver access. The pod was now a simple half oval, keeping the large speedometer and tachometer, but the temperature and fuel gauges moved to the top center for instant reading. The best part was the center console, which was canted slightly toward the driver but within easy reach of the rider.

HVAC (heater, vent, air-conditioning) push-button controls were within easy reach with the radio riding just below. Best of all was the new adjustable steering column that let you move the wheel right where you wanted it. Gone, however, was the cubby on top of the dash, but there was a slot ahead of the shifter to move that stuff into. Lights and wipers still were found on the same stalks.

While both old and new dash arrays offered good looks, excellent vision and the feel of spaciousness, the 1988 design worked much better from the standpoint of human engineering and was more in tune with what the CRX was all about.

Steering wheel and gearshift

The other two controls critical to the operation of your CRX were the steering wheel and the shift lever, and you may want to consider replacements. Nothing fundamental was wrong with them. The wheel was well placed on the older models, and the adjustable column in the 1988 models only improved on it.

The shifter was a good-sized knob and in easy reach for any driver. The problem was that both the wheel and the shift knob were plastic, and they just were not that nice to look at or hold on to. A little more than $200 can buy you a pleasing leather wheel and shift knob from an aftermarket supplier. The frugal can get a leather wrap for the wheel or order the wrap Honda offers for 1988 CRXs.

Installing a new wheel or a wrap is easy because the steering wheel is easily removed with one center bolt. Access the bolt by removing the H symbol in the center of the wheel. Removing the wheel gives you access to both sides and a chance to get a tight stitch on the wrap. Be sure you straighten the front wheels and get the splines lined up when reinstalling so that the steering wheel is centered for driving. This may not sound like much, but you would not believe how differently you will feel about your car with a new wheel. I installed a Momo Cobra wheel, and it has given me even more new enjoyment while driving the car.

Seats and pedals

The seating position in all models was nearly perfect no matter what your size. Seat travel was plentiful on both sides and the seat recline could put you as far from the wheel and pedals as you liked to be. The secret to the CRX seat was that it was not high off the floor, which was much different than the chairlike seats in the Civics. This low position gave greater legroom.

All CRXs came with cloth seats in a two-tone pattern. The seats and interior appointments changed with each passing year. The early models had black seats with gray center inserts and moderate side bolsters. The 1986 upgrade gave the seats a black-and-gray checkered pattern insert and beefier bolstering, and by 1988 we got striped inserts with heavier bolstering yet.

Seats in the CRX improved with each revision. Seats in the first CRX had moderate side bolsters and excellent leg support.

By 1988, the bolsters had grown slightly larger, but seat construction remained basically the same.

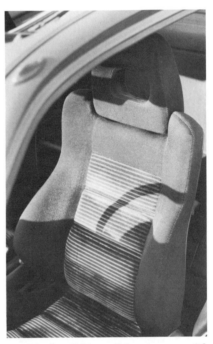

Again the 1988 model was new with taller backrests, large, stiffer side bolsters and large leg supports. Also in 1988, Honda changed the seat material to a more coarse and seemingly more durable cloth.

The seats were all comfortable for the long haul and held you fairly tight during spirited driving, although they were a little short on thigh support for taller drivers. Heavier side and hip extensions in 1988 gave you a nice tucked-in feel; however, drivers with bigger builds could have found the seatback a bit too narrow. Padding in the CRX seats was firm, and when coupled with the stiff ride, your kidneys could get jostled a bit.

Side bolsters in the pre-1988 models were minimal and provided adequate support during moderate cornering, but when you started to increase the g forces, there was not much to hold you in place. Hip support was good. The 1988 CRXs had much larger bolsters and a deeper seatwell that kept you more firmly in your seat.

Outward visibility from the driver's seat was excellent. Because of the car's diminutive size, you sat close to the windshield which allowed superior forward vision. The hood all but disappeared just beyond the top of the dashboard. Side- and rear-quarter sight was equally good.

Rear vision was a mixed bag. In pre-1988 models, a look in the rearview mirror told you all you needed; however, in backing and parking situations the tall tail hindered your sight. Some practice in learning the car's overall length helped this matter. The 1988 model added the rear glass panel below the rear window. While it may have looked a bit awkward from the outside, it was a godsend for backing and parallel parking. In earlier models, you might have found the high-mount stoplamp encroaching in the field of the rearview mirror; it was moved to the glass panel in the newer cars.

By 1988, pedal placement had not changed since we first met the CRX four years earlier. All three were lined up logically and neatly, although the brake and accelerator may have been a bit too close for true heel-toers. I found that putting the ball of my foot on the brake and cocking my heel toward the accelerator and rocking it to blip the throttle works rather well. There was not enough room for a paddle-foot like me, however, to get the proper angle on the pedals to correctly brake and rev. The footrest, an extra nicety, added to the comfort of cruising, not to men-

Pedal placement in the CRX was excellent. The brake was within easy reach of the accelerator for easy heel-toeing.

The footwell was enhanced in 1987 with the addition of a footrest. It not only was comfortable and reduced carpet wear, but it also was an excellent aid for planting your body into the seat during spirited cornering.

tion protecting the carpet. The footrest also helped make up for the lack of seat bolstering. A firmly planted foot could keep you from sliding side to side during quick maneuvers.

The throttle in the CRX was light and smooth enough that a feather touch could make all the difference. With practice you could make a multitude of adjustments in the car's speed and attitude with the tiniest inputs on the gas pedal. It was practically impossible to make the car hiccup with a jerky throttle. It was unique because the lack of feel was *actually* a feel and you could become accustomed to it. Besides, one toe on the accelerator was enough to hold a steady speed.

The clutch was an absolute delight. Operation was buttery smooth, and you could race up and down through the gears—far removed from the kick-a-rock clutches of the sports cars in the days of yore. The gearbox was equally smooth with crisp definitive gates and a nice short throw, much shorter than the previous series of Civics. I found fast upshifting could sometimes be marred by a subtle crunch as the gears met; a couple of the road testers complained of the same problem. Shifting a hair slower solved the problem.

A fully automatic transmission was available on the base CRX only. It was an excellent four-speed unit with a lock-up torque converter and really didn't take away from the power of the engine. The three-speed automatic in the pre-1986 models was not as good a design and could get pretty sloppy with age and abuse.

Sunroofs

Overall, daily driving in a CRX was a breeze, especially if you had an Si with the electric sunroof. The roof panel slid up, out and back so this ingenious design did not cut down on headroom.

The rocker switch controlling the sunroof had two positions giving you two options. Depressing the switch halfway tipped the rear of the roof up about an inch to provide excellent ventilation. Pushing the switch all the way down sent the roof panel up and out giving you about a $35^1/_2$ by 20 inch opening above your head. It was a clever design but seemed a bit fragile when you encountered bumpy road surfaces. In the open position the roof made quite a clatter, but it was securely attached.

When the roof was open, a small air deflector popped up. It kept the breeze and bugs from messing up your hair and still allowed plenty of airflow into the car. If you found it too windy or noisy, you could affix a sunroof visor to the car, but it did reduce the already narrow opening.

Wind noise was not obtrusive when driving with the windows down and roof open, so you didn't have to blast the radio or yell to be heard. Tooling around town with the windows up and roof open was pleasant, especially on cool clear nights, but at high speeds you got an annoying buffeting from the opening above.

The sunroof tracks become dirty quickly as dust and grime sticks to the grease. This could affect the operation of the mechanism and even cause the roof to stick. To avoid this, you should wipe down the tracks and apply more grease once or twice a year depending on how often the roof is open. Make sure you clean it well and reapply plenty of lubricant; basic petroleum jelly will suffice. An occasional shot of spray lubricant helps during the interim. Use a stem on the nozzle to avoid spray spots and stains on the paint.

One of the best features in any CRX Si. Honda found a way to provide an electric sunroof without reducing headroom or having a sliver of an opening. The sunroof slides up and out, leaving a large opening. A wind deflector pops up to cut wind noise. The roof can also be canted at the rear to allow better ventilation in the car.

Not surprisingly, the other CRX models are popular targets for aftermarket sunroofs. Some dealers even offer to put them in for you. Make sure you ask how it is installed and if any guarantees against leakage accompany the sunroof. Also be sure that the sunroof has a fairly thin frame, preferably no more than 1¼ inches thick, so you don't lose headroom. These aftermarket roofs offer one benefit that is not available to Si owners: a glass panel. I have often wished I had a glass roof, especially in poor weather. On the other hand, the insulated steel panel keeps the winter cold from coming in while the glass does not.

Sound systems

The CRX and the rest of the Honda line offered tremendous flexibility in choosing a sound system. Honda offered four radio and speaker combinations depending on your budget, all of which looked and sounded good. Your options included a basic AM/FM radio or the radio and one of three levels of tape player as well as an equalizer. A speaker in each door or a four-way system with the additional speakers mounted above the rear wheelwells was also available. They were all good decks delivering good power and sound, and the wires and speaker recesses in the car meant it was just a matter of plugging in the deck of your choice.

Ease of installation also allows sound aficionados to run down to the local hi-fi outlet and pop in something fancy. You usually can get more for your money by going this route, and you have many more options. If you install your system, you can save more headaches by purchasing a kit to adapt the power and speaker wires from the deck to the harness already in the car. It is a simple set of wires and plug you can pick up for about $10.

Honda left ample space for just about any radio and tape player on the market. If you are a purist and like things to match, such as having your instrument lights and your radio lights the same color, you will have to hunt down a radio with red-orange illumination. I have found that Sony, Technics, Kenwood and Blaupunkt will suit.

The other decision is a DIN mount stereo versus a conventional model. The simple difference is that the DIN style features one round knob for power and volume and digital push-buttons for the stations; the conventional style gives you a knob for power and volume and another for station selection. For pre-1988 models I suggest a push-button radio since it is not in easy reach and fumbling with the dial causes you to take your eyes off the road. Nearly all manufacturers offer DIN mount systems.

Don't forget the antenna. They cost $10 to $20, and it is simple to snake the wire down the windshield post and over to the radio. Speakers are also easily installed in the doors since the wires and screw holes are already provided. Speakers of 4¼ inch diameter pop into the door panels in less than an hour, but take care when removing the panels. Breaking or losing the plastic pins will leave the panels loose and rattling. If you like a bigger sound and the rear recesses do not provide enough room, you can easily cut into the side panels just below the window to accommodate six-by-nine-inch speakers. Purists who prefer not to cut up their cars can run wires to the rear and use the new portable speaker packs. They deliver great sound but are difficult to secure and are a target for theft.

The hottest ticket in car stereos in recent times has been the compact disc player. They can easily be installed in the CRX. However, they are sensitive instruments, and the short wheelbase and firm ride could easily cause the player to skip or jam.

Car stereo theft is a big problem these days and purchasing a super system can make you a target. Make sure your insurance policy covers aftermarket stereo systems. There are also a number of stereo decks available with slide mounts that allow you to pop it out of the dash and take it with you for security. These fit right into the existing opening and you can hardly tell that the stereo is removable.

Insurance

Unfortunately, insuring a CRX is like insuring a Corvette: an ordeal. No matter how much you plead with your insurance company, it will rate the car as a sports car. Many agents will not insure sports cars and will tell you to shop elsewhere. If the firm will insure sports cars, there will be an automatic 15 to 25 percent surcharge tacked on to your premium. Several reasons lie behind the high cost. The CRX is considered to have high rates for repair work and replacement parts, and because it has plastic body panels, the insurance business views the car as susceptible to greater damage in collisions. Just imagine what the effect is on Corvette and Fiero owners!

What to do? Well, if you are adding the CRX to an existing policy with other cars, your insurance agent will not send you packing, but do expect to pay quite a bit more than you had been for ordinary vehicles. The small independent companies will not accept the risk so you are best off looking to the larger firms.

Maintenance

Comments on maintenance are few because, as with all Hondas, there is not much to do. In order to get maximum enjoyment from your CRX, make sure you follow the checkup and maintenance guidelines that came with the car. Yes, it runs fine and starts all the time, but that's not the point. You can trust your tune-ups and oil changes to your corner service station as long as it employs competent mechanics. The service intervals should be left to a Honda mechanic; they cover things such as valve adjustment and checking over the entire car. It does not sound like much, but the car does run better afterward.

If you are going to do your own maintenance, don't wait until 7,500 miles for the first tune-up and oil change. I go about 2,500 for oil and 4,000 for plugs and air filter—and that's plenty. Changing your oil frequently will add years to the life of your motor. While on the subject of oil, it is *important* to use the proper oil in your CRX. The engine is designed with tight clearances and requires 5W-30 weight oil, especially in colder climates. In warm weather regions, 10W-30 can be used, but the 5W-30 is still best.

Summary

The CRX is far more complex than you may have thought. There's more to it than a potent engine in a lightweight bodyshell. Knowing about the car can only enhance your enjoyment.

What's next? Honda is not giving away any secrets, but don't be surprised if the current European version of the CRX comes to the United States soon. Now that the CRX is no longer tied to the Civic line, we could see bold new cars from Honda that could really knock the socks off some European supercars. As my friend with the 1988 CRX Si put it: "Some more power and better brakes and I'd never consider a Ferrari again."

Not a spy photo of a secret new Honda. This CRX conversion was spotted on a California freeway. No doubt the car is even more appealing with the top down.

Chapter 4

Accord
Honda reaches a new accord

In 1976, Civic sales were booming. The low-priced economy car with the CVCC engine was the perfect solution to rising gas prices. Honda added a 1500 cc engine for that model year to offer more power to the Civics yet still deliver miserly fuel economy figures.

Everyone had grown accustomed to the little Civic coupes when Honda surprised the world with a grown-up, upscale economy car powered by a new larger engine. Meet the Honda Accord. The car was introduced midyear and enjoyed almost immediate success. The popularity was so great the dealers marked up the price on the Accords some $1,000 to $1,500 and the public was willing to pay the premium.

As with all Honda debut models, customers had to contend with waiting lists and not being able to test drive the car. In 1988, this was still a factor as new models were rationed to dealers. This was an unfortunate situation and no doubt alienated many potential Honda buyers. My father was shopping for a car in 1976 and narrowed his choice to the Accord and a Toyota SR5 Liftback. While he would much rather have had the Honda, we ended up with a Toyota because we didn't have to pay extra or wait for the car.

Honda took a step up from the Civic with the debut of the 1976 Accord. The first series of cars only came in two-door hatchback trim. The Accord was so popular that there was a waiting list for the cars, and dealers were charging a premium to boot.

First generation, 1976–81

Only one model of Accord was available in the inaugural year: the hatchback. Except for the CVCC badge on the grille, no letter or model designations appeared on the car.

The new model was much larger than anything before it from Honda, or at least it appeared that way. The Accord had a wheelbase of nearly ninety-four inches which was three inches larger than the new Civic four-door, and the Accord was an inch wider at sixty-four inches. However, the car stood a full inch shorter than the Civic.

The Accord was a much more attractive car than the stubby Civic. The slightly longer wheelbase and the window treatment gave the car a bigger look, and the lines of the body were finished rather than chopped off as on the Civic.

The Accord's claim to fame was its list of options and its low price tag. Just $7,000 bought you the plushest Honda offered to date. Obviously, this model did not compare with the later Accords, but it was quite a step above the Civic. The little things made the difference: intermittent wipers, rear-window washer and wiper, rear-window defogger, remote release for the rear hatch, clock, lighted glovebox, tachometer and, of course, the coin box.

The Accord also came standard with a light-up ideogram telling you if the doors and rear hatch were ajar and if the taillights were in working order. A unique element on the fascia was the maintenance reminder. Three little lights at the bottom of the speedometer were triggered by mileage. They signified when it was time to change the oil and oil filter and rotate the tires. The remainder of the warning lights ran across the top of the display pod.

The center of the dash was occupied by the heater and vent controls and the radio. A shelf-like area ran across the top of the dash, but nothing kept items from rolling around while you drove.

The seats were vinyl with a softer insert material that could breathe to keep passengers from getting too warm. Surprisingly, the rear seats did not fold down in the early editions, and cargo space was somewhat limited. Headroom and legroom in the rear were also limited and best left for children.

Mechanically, the Accord was also much more advanced than its predecessors. Under the hood was a 1600 cc CVCC engine pushing 68 hp at 5000 rpm. This was the same powerplant found in the Civics with the addition of a slightly larger bore and stroke. A three-barrel downdraft carburetor fed the fuel. This new Honda was supported by a rather simple form of four-wheel independent suspension consisting of MacPherson struts and coil springs at all four corners, and fitted with thirteen-inch stamped steel wheels.

Standard equipment included a five-speed manual gearbox, but the Hondamatic could be substituted at additional charge. This was the same two-speed, semi-automatic transmission found in the Civics. It is hard to imagine ordering this option in an upscale car; however, the Hondamatic was able to make the car move quite well. First gear could be used all the way up to 50 mph which was especially handy for merging in traffic or climbing steep grades. Otherwise, second gear could be engaged anytime after 20 mph.

Keeping with Honda's formula, nothing was changed for the 1977 model year, but in 1978 an LX version was added. This was simply a trim package featuring goodies like air conditioning, nicer seats and door panels, power steering, sport steering wheel, fold-down rear seat and specified Michelin radials over the B. F. Goodrich fitted to the base model. All the extras came at fair price too, just $1,000 more than the base Accord.

In 1979, the Accord sprouted two more doors and a trunk. The hatchback was stretched four inches to accommodate the new ports, yet oddly enough the new model weighed just ten pounds more than the hatchback.

Standard equipment on the four-door read the same as the base hatchback, with the exception of power steering and what Honda called Custom Moquette Fabric. It sounds rather exotic but is just a fuzzier cloth. One interesting feature was the remote-control rear-door locks activated by a small lever next to the parking brake. A light on the dash signaled when the doors were unlocked. Front-door locks remained manual. The trunk offered security for parcels that would otherwise be visible in the hatchback.

All the Accords received a new 1751 cc engine that now produced 75 hp at 4500 rpm. Again, Honda had increased the bore and stroke of the 1600 cc engine to get the greater displacement. Keep in mind, this was originally the 1500 cc engine, which first received an increased stroke, then a larger bore and stroke combination. The car retained the same three-barrel downdraft carburetor.

The year 1980 gave us the same trio of Accords with the same option packages, with the exception of Honda's first fully automatic transmission. It was a three-speed unit based on the old Hondamatic two-speed and naturally was Honda's own design. Rather than using the planetary geartrain found in most auto transmissions, Honda's was designed

After four years of immense popularity, Honda took the next logical step and added two more doors to the Accord. The four-door car debuted in the fall of 1978 as a 1979 model and marked the first time a Honda had a conventional trunk.

The one shortcoming in the first series of Accords: susceptibility to rust. The biggest problem area was the inner and outer front fenders where the rust would become so bad the shock towers could cave in.

around a series of automatically engaging clutches that responded to speed. Simply put, it was a manual transmission that shifted by itself.

As you accelerated, the transmission would shift up through the gears and similarly downshift during deceleration. You could manually select second, which kept it from moving up to third, but you could not lock into first.

A passing, or kick-down, gear was easily accessed by pushing the pedal to the floor. This would drop the transmission into second, and once you let off, it shifted back to third. A light on the tachometer reminded you what gear you were in.

The base hatchback, LX hatchback and four-door sedan continued through 1981, the final year for the first-series Accords.

Looking back on the first generation and what it was like to live with them, one thing leaps to mind right away: rust. Corrosion got the best of the early Accords, and once infected, there was no saving them from the cancer. The front clip was the first to go, and unfortunately it went farther than the external fenders: the unibody was highly susceptible to rot. If you see an old Accord with serious front fender rust, it won't be long before the shock towers cave in. Once they go, you might as well throw the car away because fixing it will be either impossible or expensive.

A friend of mine had a 1977 Accord hatchback with serious cancer. On a trip to Colorado, the right shock tower caved in toward the engine. The car was his only way home so he had to devise a repair. His solution was to chain the broken shock to a phone pole and use a come-along to right it. Then he bolted a steel bar to the top, ran the bar over the motor and bolted it to the good shock, thus keeping them opposed. Not good for handling but drivable.

Inside you found all kinds of wear as well. As stated earlier, the Japanese could not seem to get carpet right in the 1970s. It would come up and come apart. Seat stitching was also victim to wear. It was too bad this happened to Honda's first big car attempt, not only because so many Accords were sold but also because it seemed like such a good car.

I say good car in the general sense. Styling was nice; it was practical, easy on gas and had many pleasant appointments. Unfortunately the shortcomings prevailed: rust problems, an underpowered engine and adequate handling.

Honda designed the car to be an affordable, economical family car, and it was exactly that. Perfect for the American family with 2.2 children and enough room for their gear. The Accord was far from a performance machine because it was a fairly heavy car weighing a bit over 2,200 lb. and only had 75 hp to move it.

Cornering was equally poor because the car severely understeered with no feel in the wheel at all, especially in the power-assisted version. The little thirteen-inch radials, even the Michelins, howled in a tight corner and felt as if they were coming off the rims while the rest of the suspension was going to fold up on the spot. This is a perfect example of what we learned with the CRX. In this case, the car weighed much more and had weaker suspension which meant even more load on the outboard tire. The tires' threshold of performance was exceeded almost immediately. An upgraded tire would have quickly helped the situation but was only worth it if the car was clean and going to last you a while.

Second generation, 1982–85

Honda learned from its problems and brought us the second-generation Accord in 1982. The car retained the same shape but got a facelift both inside and out. The lines took on a more square appearance; a new grille featured four square headlights in place of the four round lights of the previous issue. New taillights were added, and the bumpers were integrated into the body design.

Inside were new seats and a new dash layout. The Accord was still chock full of those standard features that had made a name for the car, right down to the maintenance reminder and the door-ajar map telling you if the doors or hatch were open. Mechanically everything remained the same, as did the models offered: hatchback, LX hatchback and sedan.

True to form, the Accords carried over for 1983, with the exception of a Special Edition model. This SE came packed with all the luxury options of the LX plus a power moonroof, leather seats and leather trim inside, special steering wheel and new road wheels. The car came only in dark gray with gray leather interior. Sale price on the SE was in the neighborhood of $11,000, while the rest of the Accords hovered around $8,300. This marked the first Honda to break the $10,000 barrier.

The SE was only available in 1983, and in 1984 Honda returned to the old Accord trio with the addition of an LX sedan. The LX gave you a few more standard niceties including air conditioning, leather-wrapped steering wheel and power moonroof.

Honda brought back the Accord foursome in 1985, and only minor changes had taken place. Honda also renewed the Special Edition, but this time the beauty was more than skin deep. Along with the leather seats, sliding roof and alloy wheels came a fuel-injected engine that gave the car an extra letter designation. The SEi featured the same 1800 cc, 110 hp motor as the Prelude, as well as four-wheel disc brakes. These cosmetic and performance goodies brought the SEi up to a new class of cars, nearly comparable to the Euro sedans—yet the Accord only cost $12,000.

As with all of Honda's product lines, the car was to run its course for several years with only minor changes. Then Honda would unveil an entirely new car with restyled body panels, new suspension and new options. In 1982, the Accord was reborn with new sheet metal, longer wheelbase, new engine and new interior appointments.

The second series of Accords came during Honda's emphasis on square elements in the design. The car had a boxy appearance, and the two round headlamps in the first series gave way to four square lights. All Hondas carried square headlamps from this point on.

This series improved greatly on the first editions. Honda licked the rust problems with some undercoating, plastic fenderwell liners and antichip paint on the lower bodyside. The second-generation Accords were also better-mannered road cars because they were smoother, quieter and quicker, especially the SEi version. Both the base models and the Special Editions made excellent family and commuter cars. The sedan had ample room for four adults to travel comfortably, and the folding rear seat enhanced cargo capacity.

Again, the 1985 Accord was not designed for performance, but was much improved over the previous line-up. Understeer was still prevalent, but better tires and a little firmer suspension kept you from feeling as if you were running the tires off the rims. The independent suspension easily sucked up the bumps but did clunk on the deep holes and lumps.

Torque-steer was still not a problem since the car didn't really have enough power to pull the wheel in either direction. This was not to say the car was underpowered; rather, the power was closely matched with the car and its purpose.

Third generation, 1986
Honda's family car had progressed toward the ranks of the low-end European sedans like the 320 BMWs and 190 Mercedes, and the third generation made the big step into luxury. The 1986 Accords were com-

The 1982 Prelude four-door front grille.

The 1984 Prelude four-door grille with subtle changes.

The 1985 Prelude four-door grille. The grate in the bumper of the 1984 and 1985 models was for show only.

67

pletely redone from the ground up, with new suspension, drivetrain, skin and guts. The Special Editions were also incorporated into the regular line-up.

"Alphabet soup" was the best way to describe the new series of Accords. Honda added a letter designation to the base model calling it DX, while the upscale version retained LX and the top-of-the-line Accord (formerly known as the Special Edition) was now LXi.

All three models got the new double wishbone suspension at both ends with front stabilizer bars. Only the LXi models got rear stabilizers. This provided a smoother and quieter ride because suspension travel allowed the chassis to soak up more of the impact and transmit less to the cockpit. A coil spring was incorporated into the rear suspension to preserve ride height and attitude. The design also prevented diving under hard braking and lifting during acceleration.

The gang also got the new two-liter, twelve-valve engine rated at 98 hp at 3500 rpm in the carbureted version and 110 hp at 4500 rpm with fuel injection. Torque was also bumped up to 109 lb-ft and 114 lb-ft respectively. Each version came standard with Honda's five-speed or an optional four-speed automatic.

Cosmetically, the car had also been completely redone. This was by far Honda's most aerodynamic Accord as well as its prettiest. All the panels were lowered and rounded for minimum wind resistance, and the front end sported pop-up headlights. The double wishbone suspension took up far less room under the car, allowing for a lower hood and rear deck while creating more interior room.

The fascia had been totally revamped and resembled the Integra's in many ways. Three large circles shaded by a hood faced the driver. The tachometer and speedometer got their own space, while the temperature and gas gauges shared the right-most dial. The two smaller needles were also accompanied by Accord's patented door-ajar lights and a gear indicator for cars equipped with the automatic.

Push-button HVAC controls were located at the center of the dash, and the radio occupied the lower-most portion of the panel. Seats, carpet,

The coming of double-wishbone suspension dramatically changed the look of the Accord in 1987. The car took on a sleek appearance with a lower hood *line and smoother lines from front to rear. The pop-up headlamps were remarkable, similar in design to the Prelude.* Honda

door panels and headliners were covered in the most plush materials ever seen in a Honda—similar to the treatment in the Integra LS. The texture of the fabrics changed as you went up through the ranks, with the LXi version being the snappiest. The split, fold-down rear seat also featured a folding armrest and shoulder belts. There was plenty of room for two or three adults to ride comfortably in the rear, and the folding seat allowed access to the trunk or provided more cargo space in the sedan or hatchback.

Luxury options such as power windows, moonroof, power mirrors and alloy wheels were only available on the LXi version. The rest of the line-up got things like wheel covers and manually operated mirrors, but most of the trim goodies could be added by the dealer. Little was offered or needed for the LXi.

The year 1987 was another carryover, and 1988 was more or less a carryover as well, with some minor additions and deletions. In 1988, the midrange LX hatchback was dropped from the line-up reducing the Accord selection to five models. The big news was that the fuel-injected models got a ten percent boost in horsepower pushing them up to 120 hp, plus new 60 series Michelin MXVs mounted on fourteen-inch wheels. The rest of the Accords kept their 98 hp carbureted engines and thirteen-inch wheels. The car was still fairly thrifty with fuel mileage rating in the mid-twenties in town and upper thirties on the highway. Honda also added stronger body and chassis members, center pillars and suspension mounting points for a more solid, quiet ride.

A number of trim and option changes accounted for the rest of the differences in the 1988 Accords. These included passive-restraint seatbelts, speed-sensitive power steering and timed rear defroster. New stereo options included compact disc and power antenna.

The dash display of the third series of Accords. The fascia had come a long way from the first edition. Although the 1988 Accord dash was still made of plastic, it had a softer look to it. Notice the number of comfort amenities, such as electric windows, cruise control, AM/FM cassette stereo and air conditioning, making it the Cadillac of Hondas. Honda

Seats in the third series of Accords were the best to date. Note the large side and thigh bolsters for extra support and a Recaro-like appearance. Accord seats were covered in a soft velour-like fabric with a more durable fabric insert. Honda

The speed-sensitive, variable-assist power steering automatically adjusted tension on the steering rack based on inputs from the engine. At low speeds and parking situations, it allowed you to turn the wheels with minimal effort, and in rambunctious cornering, it stiffened to better communicate what was happening at the wheels. At moderate speeds, steering was easy with adequate road feel.

Honda's biggest news on the Accord front came about midyear with the debut of the new Accord coupe. This striking new coupe was the first two-door Accord to offer a trunk rather than a hatchback. The coupe came in two trim levels: DX and LXi. As always, the base model got the short end of the stick on options, while the upscale edition was overflowing with standard equipment.

Wheelbase on the new coupe was the same as on the rest of the Accords, as were the engine and transmission options. The DX came with the carburetors and 98 hp, and the LXi received the 120 horses of fuel-injected power. The interiors also offered the same layout and appointments as on other models.

The coupe was the sexiest Accord on the roads, but the real story behind the coupe was in manufacturing. This was the first Honda built solely in the United States and exported throughout the world, including Japan—truly a milestone in foreign-domestic automobile manufacturing.

Power was the same in the base models: adequate. The extra horses in the fuel-injected models were a welcome improvement and surprisingly evident when surrounded by all that luxury. Performance was good, and the engine revved nicely all the way to the red zone. The five-speed was smooth and precise as always, but one might have thought

Honda debuted an all-new Accord coupe in 1988. This was the first Accord two-door with a conventional trunk. The platform met the Prelude head on, although the Accord was less expensive. This led to speculation of an all-new Prelude in the offing. The Accord coupe was only produced in the United States and exported to Japan. Honda

that the comfort factor called for an automatic. The four-speed auto was smooth and quiet, but the manual gearbox provided much more fun.

As far as ergonomics went, what was not to like? The 1988 Accords offered all the plushness and comfort of Lincolns and Cadillacs but without overstating the luxury and without the marshmallow ride.

The addition of fourteen-inch wheels and 60 series tires made a noticeable improvement in handling. The Accords still understeered a bit, but the stabilizer bars reduced vertical load in the front wheels, and the tires had a much higher level of performance.

There is little or nothing you could or would want to add to the Accords, especially the 1988 version. As with all Hondas, it is simple to install your own stereo equipment. Speaker wiring is already in place, and there is ample room for a tape deck. A sunroof is always nice to have, and a number of places can outfit your Accord without much effort or expense.

Summary

The Accord has come a long way since its debut in 1976. Fit and finish have improved immensely as has the standard equipment. It was hard to say whether the Accord was still that inexpensive, economical family car when prices have crept over $15,000, but when you considered what you got for your dollar, it was a good value.

What is next for the Accord? Many possibilities exist. In 1988, the Europeans got a model of the Accord called Aerodeck. The car was basically the Accord hatchback with an elongated roofline which made it look like a station wagon.

The car came in two trim levels: EX and EX 2.0i. Both cars were powered by a 1955 cc, four-cylinder engine with the latter receiving Honda's

An Accord station wagon? Not quite. Pictured is the 1988 Aerodeck EX, which was a restyled hatchback version of the Accord. This model was not available in the United States. Honda had contemplated marketing the Aerodeck in the United States, but then felt there would not be a market for it. Could they have been wrong? Honda

71

PGM fuel-injection. The 2.0i pumped out 122 hp at 5500 rpm while the carbureted version peaked at 106 hp. Suspension was the same four-wheel double wishbone found in domestic cars, but the 2.0i featured four-wheel, anti-lock disc brakes. Honda has named their braking system ALB II. The EX had front discs with rear drums.

One of the most interesting engineering features in the Aerodeck was the hydraulic engine mounts to reduce vibration. This also helped reduce increased engine vibration as the car got older because jack-rabbit starts caused the engine to rock, further increasing wear on the mounts.

The interior was identical to the rest of the Accord line-up for 1988. However, in this case there was much more cargo capacity which was enhanced by the folding rear seat.

As Accords progress toward that world class status and away from the family orientation, look for more options and performance. It cannot be long before the four-wheel, anti-lock disc brakes and sixteen-valve engines come to the world market, and the Honda clock shows the car is due for some styling revisions as well. New performance extras will no doubt appear first on the new coupe before the rest of the line-up. Perhaps the Aerodeck will also come to America.

Chapter 5

Prelude
Stepping toward sports

In 1979, Honda introduced its Sports Car for Adults: the Prelude. It was an odd name for a car ten years ago but today rolls off the tongue a bit easier than Diahatsu or Hyundai. Honda's pronunciation, by the way, is "prey-lude" although you have no doubt heard it called "prel-ude" and "pre-lude."

How Honda derived the term sports car from the 1979 Prelude remains a question. The styling was typical of 1970s Japanese design: small, boxy and with some unique elements. The two-door coupe had squared-off front and rear with a slightly rounded corner to the roofline. The lines were clean, straight and simple, yet the grille and headlight assembly did not seem to go with the rest of the car—nor did the taillights. It was almost a combination of elements popular in US cars put into a smaller shape, things like square headlights and flush-mounted door handles similar to mid-1970s AMC cars. The high-cut fenderwells made the car look too big for the wheels.

All in all, nothing about the car's styling, appearance or performance said sports car. This was especially true when you considered the im-

Styling on the inaugural Prelude of 1979 was typical of Japanese design in the 1970s: choppy and stubby. The powerplant of the first Preludes matched its rather sedate design, and the car was given the nickname Qualude by many.

ported Asian sports cars the Prelude was up against: the Datsun 280Z and the Mazda RX-7. By 1979, both competitors had made names for themselves with sexy styling, kick-in-the-pants performance and a relatively low price.

Indeed, the Prelude not only lacked the lines of the Mazda and the Z-car, it also was missing the powerful drivetrain and the tough-guy suspension. This lack of performance was undoubtedly the reason the Honda was nicknamed the Qualude by many. Simply put, the Prelude lacked the punch and pizzazz you normally associate with a sports car, and even with its backseat it was difficult to imagine it as a GT or 2 + 2.

I'm not going to condemn the car as a marketing mistake because it was really a comfortable car. No one chastized Honda for calling it a sports car, and Honda sold a ton of them. I even wanted to own one when they arrived. Unfortunately, I was a poor college student with meager means and only a clapped-out Opel GT to my name.

A bird's-eye view of the Prelude's most popular standard feature. The electric moonroof was a smoked glass panel that slid back into the headliner. The roof was electric, and a sun shield could be manually slid into place with the roof closed. A small air and bug deflector automatically popped up when the roof was open.

The rear of the first Preludes was stubby. Here is an example of 1970s Japanese styling with an oddly shaped taillight integrating the stop lamp, turn indicator and reverse lamp.

Seats in the first series were upgraded versions of Civic seats. They offered little lateral support, but had plenty of leg space. They sported cloth inserts for a more upscale appearance.

74

First generation, 1979–82

The common thread that tied the Prelude to its contemporaries was also its strongest selling point: options. The Prelude came full boat right off the boat, all for less than $8,000. Included in the price were things like a rear-window defogger, front disc brakes, deluxe interior trim and best of all, an electric moonroof. This was a prestigious piece of standard equipment for an economy car and gave the Prelude a real boost in the credibility department. Even the Datsun 280Z and Mazda RX-7 could only offer removable roof panels.

The Prelude's moonroof dropped down and slid back inside the rear section of the roof above the backseats. It was a good-sized opening measuring 20 1/2 inches across and thirty-five inches front to back. The real nicety of the electric moonroof was that it was a glass panel rather than a removable steel panel as offered in the RX-7. Although the Datsun featured a glass T-top, having one required stopping the car, futzing with the T-top bag and strapping it down in the rear.

Prelude owners could open and shut their roofs with a mere press of a button, without missing a beat in traffic. An added bonus in the Prelude was the sliding moonroof cover in the headliner. This shielded the passengers from the hot rays of the sun or from the chill of the glass panel in the colder months.

The only drawback to the overhead opening was that it reduced headroom a bit. Taller drivers and passengers had a tough time fitting, and backseat riders had to tilt their heads or study their shoes for the course of the journey. Unfortunately for some, the slider was a standard feature that forced them to change their driving position or look for another car.

The interior was the most plush of any Honda to date. Thicker carpeting covered the floors, and the seats were tailored in a nice cloth. The front seats sported moderate side bolsters, wider and more comfortable thigh support and four-way adjustable headrests. A small console split the front buckets. The rear was a bench seat covered in the same velourlike cloth.

Just as the exterior styling had its curiosities, so did the dashboard. Seated behind the wheel, you found everything within easy reach and more or less pleasing to the eye—until you looked into the driver's information center. Staring back at you was a cyclops speedometer and tachometer spinning off the same axis. Speed was checked on the larger outer dial and revs ticked off the inner circle. Idiot lights were positioned at the base of the gauge: left of the big dial were the fuel and temperature gauges; to the right was the maintenance reminder and a digital clock.

The intent behind this unique instrument cluster was to provide large, easy-to-read gauges in one compact space. Nevertheless, it was one of the oddest features in a Honda car, and this dashboard only lasted two model years.

The exterior styling was suspect as well, especially at a time when Honda's contemporaries were building exciting sports coupes. The Prelude was an upscale, sporty coupe more or less aimed at that market. It was not ugly, yet it was not exciting either. The Prelude was vanilla in a world of double brownie delights.

The first Prelude's styling fit the epitome of the term econobox. The lines of the entire car were squared-off, especially at the front and rear where the car seemed to end abruptly. The high-cut fenderwells left the thirteen-inch tires looking like inner tubes floating in the Sea of Japan. The design was hardly a result of state-of-the-art wind tunnel testing.

Interestingly enough, the debut model offered the first conventional trunk on a Honda—albeit small, it was still a trunk. Not until the next generation did the rear seat fold down to offer more cargo space.

The unusual concentric tachometer and speedometer in the early first-series Preludes. Both instruments spun on the same axis with a group of warning lights in the center. Honda's theory was safety so that the driver would only have to look in one place. Temperature and fuel gauges were at the left and a driver information center at the right.

Radio dials and knobs were also unique in the early first-series Preludes. The large knob on the side of the pod changed stations, and the concentric knobs at the front controlled volume and tone. The tape deck was below on the lower portion of the dash. If concentric gauges were for safety, this radio certainly was not. Also note the four-spoked, uninspiring steering wheel carried over from the Civic.

It did not take Honda long to realize the shortcomings of the dash, and in 1982 it debuted a more conventional arrangement. The pod was enlarged to separate the speedometer and tachometer, and the radio and tape deck were united at the lower center of the fascia.

The 1751 cc CVCC engine in the first-series Preludes was not powerful enough to lift the car to the sports car level. Some of this lack of power could be attributed to the pollution control, exhibited with all of its power-robbing hoses visible here.

Under the square hood sat the same 1751 cc CVCC engine that powered the Accord. It is interesting to note in today's age of mega-valves for performance and efficiency that the 1981 version of the 1751 cc engine featured three valves per cylinder, with two for intake and one larger valve for exhaust. Coupling this with the three-barrel carburetor brought net horsepower to a meager 75 at 3500 rpm.

As usual you could have the engine bolted to the five-speed manual or the optional Hondamatic transmission. Suspension was also the same as in the Accord with independent MacPherson struts and coil springs at the corners. Both cars boasted rack-and-pinion steering.

The Prelude remained basically unchanged through 1982, with the exception of the revamped dashboard in 1981. The new dash looked similar to the old but appeared to flow much better, and the concentric speedometer and tachometer were separated into two large dials.

All in all, Honda's first attempt at a GT car was not too far off the mark, but the company was about to do better.

A unique Prelude. This late first-series model was converted to a convertible by a firm in Germany. The rear seat was removed to make room for the top assembly. The owner claims only four Preludes were converted by this firm; three are in the United States. Note this car sports Honda's luggage rack.

Second generation, 1983-87

As quickly as you could say Cinderella, a new Prelude appeared in 1983. This new car bore no resemblance to its predecessor whatsoever: an aerodynamic wedge shape replaced the old square body. The new Prelude also got a new engine and new suspension.

The old 1751 cc CVCC engine was replaced by a new 1829 cc engine that also featured a cast-iron block and aluminum head. The new engine now burned unleaded fuel even though it utilized the CVCC aluminum head. The engine also featured two one-barrel Keihin carburetors rather

The second-generation Prelude debuted in 1983 and offered a much more sleek, refined look. No elements from the first series carried over into the new edition. The sunroof was offered on all Preludes as standard equipment.

Part of the restyling and sleek new look incorporated pop-up headlamps, which gave the Prelude more of an exotic appeal. These were some of the most reliable pop-up lights offered on an automobile. According to dealers, Honda headlamps have had minimal instances of winking, where one light stays open.

than the old solo three-barrel. This boosted horsepower twenty-five percent to an even 100 hp.

The increased power gave the Prelude a real lift in performance
since the redesigned car gained only sixty-two pounds in its metamorphosis. Now 0–60 mph came in just under ten ticks, but the performance
faded quickly, taking over seventeen seconds to complete a quarter-mile.
The Prelude was controlled by a five-speed manual or three-speed automatic with lock-up torque converter.

The most unique element of the new Prelude was the suspension system that, once again, was an original Honda design. The designers
wanted the car to have more of a sports coupe look, requiring a lower
hoodline and nose. So out with the ubiquitous MacPherson struts and in
with Honda's new A-arm/strut suspension. It was quite ingenious and a
bit complicated but achieved the same result as the typical upper and
lower A-arm suspension.

The rear end kept the Chapman struts and trailing arms from the
previous model. Brakes were also the same as in the first Prelude with
discs up front and drums in the rear. Honda introduced a four-disc system in Europe and Japan that same year.

Cosmetically, the car looked more like a sports car but retained a lot
of its sedan lines. The car was bigger and taller with larger doors, a bigger
trunk and new pop-up headlights, but not as racy as the Z or RX-7. Considering comfort and convenience, it rivaled the BMW 320i and Mazda
626.

When you saw the old and new cars together, the 1983 model truly
looked and felt larger, but the numbers were not so different. Wheelbase
had only stretched out to 96 1/2 inches from ninety-one inches, and the
overall length grew just nine inches from the original 161. The new sheet
metal made for a surprisingly smaller surface area on the roof thus reducing the size of the Prelude's trademark moonroof. The resized opening
measured 18 1/4 by thirty-five inches.

A plumber's nightmare. The second se-
ries of Preludes was powered by a
twelve-valve, dual-carburetor engine.
It is plain to see why it is best to have a
Honda mechanic work on this engine.

Inside, the car got an entire makeover as well. The same four instruments prevailed in perfect view with large numerals and needles for quick reference. Wipers and lights were again operated from stalks on the column.

You selected HVAC settings via pneumatic push buttons, and a sliding lever operated the progressive-speed fan. Your choice of radio fit just below the climate controls which also fed vents along the top of the door panels for side-window defrosting. Small swiveling vents in the door panels provided heat or cool air to the passengers. A small console divided the new cloth seats.

The seats were a godsend in comparison to those in the former Prelude. The reclining front buckets sported new lumbar supports and side bolsters that held you snugly in place. The bolsters were a little stiff, and some may find them uncomfortable. The plush new velourlike cloth covering the front and rear seats and door panels gave a much more luxurious appearance that was associated with upscale GT cars.

The backseats had more legroom and headroom, but it was still a bit confining for adults. The best feature of the new rear seats was a folding seatback that allowed access to the trunk and more cargo space. The seatback also locked, keeping belongings relatively safe if the car was left unlocked. The remote releases for the trunk and fuel door also locked.

The Prelude was truly transformed and could now go to the ball with the rest of the sports cars. There was only one blemish: Honda molded fake stitching into the dashboard, and it was out of synch with the rest of the car.

Honda was obviously happy with the changes to the Prelude, and since it was so busy unveiling the new CRXs and Civics, little happened to the Prelude during the next four years.

A revised body style called for new seats. The second-generation Preludes featured large side and leg bolsters and a funky design. Larger drivers may have found the side bolsters too confining. Cover materials changed, but the design remained the same for third-generation models.

The second-series Prelude debuted in 1983 and received a new dash display. The layout was clean and simple with a long shelf running across the dash for small items. The shifter console still did not meet the dash, and the new three-spoked steering wheel seemed unbalanced as it rotated due to the large center spoke for the horn.

In 1984, rear disc brakes, power steering and an adjustable steering column became standard. In 1985, Honda added an Si version of the Prelude. The car featured a fuel-injected, two-liter engine that kicked out ten percent more horsepower than the twin-carbureted model and had a 0–60 mph time of 9.1 seconds. Other new equipment on the Si included power windows and mirrors, cruise control, leather steering wheel, air conditioning, new corduroy upholstery and a graphic equalizer for the radio.

The Si models in 1985 featured four-wheel disc brakes, and in 1986 the base models were fitted with the same brakes. A plus? No, not exactly. In fact, *Road & Track* found them to be worse than the disc and drum combination of 1985: minimum stopping distance increased by ten percent.

As in the earlier edition, the rear deck of the Prelude ended abruptly. Taillights were much more conventional in design, and there was a slight lip on the trunk lid. This example features the optional rear deck luggage rack. It was not very functional, but did complement the look of the car.

The third-series Prelude resembled its predecessor in many ways. The overall shape and lines were much the same; however, the newer model was lower and sleeker thanks to the space-saving double-wishbone suspension. The lip on the rear deck lid also became more pronounced. Honda

The Si was easily identified by the small spoiler on the trunk lid and the new lacey spoke wheels. The Si also featured same-color upper and lower body panels, while the base model retained the gray lower panels. The base model remained unchanged.

In 1986, the cars simply got the center, high-mount brake lights required by law. Status quo for 1987.

Third generation, 1988

The year 1988 brought us the third-generation Prelude with yet another facelift and an engineering first. The new design was sleeker but not that far removed from the second phase, yet nothing was interchangeable. Most noticeable was the new hood and front-end design which was even lower than on the earlier cars. The windshield was raked a bit more, and all the glass was flush-mounted. A new lip on the trunk lid eliminated the stick-on rear spoiler of old.

Wheelbase increased by 4½ inches in keeping with the bigger and better theme, and overall length moved out 3½ inches. The 1988 Preludes came in three trim levels which corresponded to three engine options. The basic S came with a two-liter, single-cam, twelve-valve engine with dual carburetors. The base Si and four-wheel steering Si were both powered by the two-liter, twin-cam, sixteen-valve, fuel-injected engine. The base model pumped out 104 hp at 5800 rpm, while the upscale model rated 135 hp at 6200 rpm.

All three versions got the new double wishbone suspension as well as the speed-sensitive, power-assisted rack-and-pinion steering. This system varied the amount of assisting the pump did based on how much help was needed. Obviously, it was easier to steer when the car was rolling; therefore, the pump worked harder at rest.

The trio was fitted with power-assisted four-wheel disc brakes, but only the Si versions got the fourteen-inch Michelin MXV tires. The base S model still carried thirteen-inch radials.

The creamy smooth five-speed was standard, but an optional four-speed automatic was available in all three packages. The automatic featured a sport-shift button to the left of the gear selector. This allowed you two additional shifting options. The first level gave you higher shift points so you didn't have to mash the pedal to get better acceleration. The third setting simply eliminated the top gear.

Of course, while America was marveling over the new Prelude, the Japanese and Europeans were indulging in an even more advanced model as Honda debuted the 4WS 2.0i-16. This was a sixteen-valve version of the fuel-injected twelve-valve, and those extra valves brought horsepower to 150 at 6000 rpm. The regular carbureted version was rated at 114 hp at 5800 rpm. Also featured on the 2.0i-16 were four-wheel anti-lock brakes designated ALB.

If that wasn't enough, Honda also offered a limited-edition Prelude abroad in 1988. It was the 4WS version with extra goodies that came standard, including anti-lock brakes, air conditioning, leather seats front and rear, leather wrapped steering wheel and luxury cut-pile carpets.

The Si 4WS was the first production car to offer steerable rear wheels. This was not a big revelation since the technology had been around for several years, but Honda was the first to use it. The technology, not as complicated as it sounds, involved a simple mechanical system rather than electrics or hydraulics; this was to make it more reliable and cost effective. A long shaft ran from the front steering box to a steering box at the rear of the car. The rearward box reacted to input from the front box, but the front and rear wheels were not always headed in the same direction.

Here's how it worked. The rear steering rate was one-third of the front wheels' steering rate and decreased from there, so as front-wheel steering deflection increased, the rear wheels would point in the same direction. Once the steering wheel had been turned 246 degrees off the center mark, the rear wheels would be aimed straight ahead, and turning beyond that, the rear wheels turned in the opposite direction of the front wheels.

The engine bay was cleaned up immensely with the switch to fuel injection. The Preludes were the first to receive Honda's programmed fuel injection in the 1984 Si model. Pictured is the 1988 Si version.

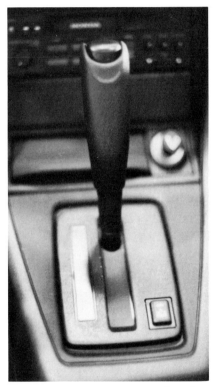

All Preludes came standard with a five-speed manual transmission. Of course, the five-speed delivered the best performance. Making an automatic transmission quicker is not always easy. In 1988, Honda offered a sport-shift button on Prelude automatics. In sport mode, the engine could get higher into the rev band before shifting, thus delivering more power without having to mash the pedal through the carpet.

83

Honda finally worked the bugs out of the poor braking in the Prelude. Minimum stopping distances dropped nearly twenty percent from the first year of four-wheel discs and were nearly ten percent shorter than with the disc and drum arrangement.

Obviously, the effect of four-wheel steering was most evident at lower speeds. The car turned quicker because the rear wheels toed out as the front wheels turned in. This made the back end come around quickly and took you by surprise the first time you encountered it. The benefit was easier maneuvering in parking lots and tight areas, as the turning circle was reduced from 33$^{1/2}$ feet to just under 31$^{1/2}$ feet, while slalom speed was increased from 61 mph to just over 65 mph.

The interior of the Si was the model of ergonomics. Everything was easy to read and easy to reach for the front-seat occupants. The dashboard wrapped around you with the important switches at your fingertips. Extraneous controls clustered in the center console.

Seating position was good and visibility was excellent. The low, sloping hood disappeared just beyond the wipers, and the large side windows gave you plenty of peripheral vision. The new, slimmer rear-roof pillars helped the rear-flank view.

The front seats were quite solid and had large side supports. The Si models came with three-position memory as well. Once again, the rear seats were no place for adults on long trips. There was minimal legroom and headroom despite the longer wheelbase.

The third-series Preludes was offered in 1988 and delivered the most ergonomic dash display of all Hondas. The center panel was raked toward the windshield, and the console was integrated into the dash. The revised three-spoked wheel was well balanced with equal spokes, and the cruise control switches were built into the right side. The new dash also delivered a total cockpit feel as the dash blended into the door panels for a wraparound feel.

Door panels in the second- and third-generation Preludes featured several convenience extras like window defrosters in the top of the panel and a swiveling vent for heat or air conditioning. Map pockets and speaker openings were standard equipment.

Driving

Putting the first-generation Prelude through its paces only reinforced the fact the car was not a sports car. It was, however, a good road car and was by far the quietest of all Hondas when on the road, with more insulation and interior appointments to absorb the sound of the tires and engine.

The motor revved freely, but the car did not exactly race through the gears, and there appeared to be more commotion than movement. Nearly eleven seconds elapsed before the needle spun to 60 mph, and the quarter-mile came along in 18½ seconds. Torque was minimal and almost unnoticeable as the car was so lacking in power.

Cornering in the first-generation Prelude was a mixed bag. The small tires and suspension layout was not capable of heavy cornering loads but the car was balanced well enough to make up for that. As with all front-drivers charging into a corner would induce an understeer but with a little finesse you could bring the rear end around. *Road & Track* described the car's handling as "nimble and better-balanced" in the hands of an experienced driver. Inexperienced drivers will find the initial understeer to be a bit alarming.

Like the first Accords, the second-generation cars received an engine that loved to cruise and rev happily. The clutch and five-speed gearbox were Honda's standard smooth-as-silk design—even the shift changes on the three- and four-speed automatics were almost undetectable. On the other hand, the brakes were a bit soft and felt as if they had barely enough power to stop the car.

Although the power-steering lacked a bit of feel, the second-series Prelude was amazingly neutral when it came to cornering. The car appeared to glide effortlessly through turns with minimal body roll and the seats keep you firmly planted even in high g's. *Road & Track* found minimal understeer and the overall characteristics to be smooth, balanced and competent. Honda's design engineers had used a Porsche 924 as their model for the Prelude and *Road & Track* determined that "they hit it dead center."

The Si was better. Road tests in the prominent car magazines applauded the car's power and roadholding capabilities. A major contributor was the Si's fourteen-inch wheels and Michelin MXV tires. (The base Prelude only got the off-the-shelf plain-Jane passenger car radial: the Bridgestone RD 116, designed to be a low-cost OE tire.) There was not that much added power in the Si version, but the extra suspension components and interior goodies were worth the small premium.

Both versions delivered effortless long-term cruising with minimal road noise and high comfort. Controls were handy, and the instruments were easy to read. Naturally, we open-air types found the power moonroof a delight. The only drawback to the Prelude was the rather stiff suspension which delivered a harder ride than you expected from a car that catered to comfort.

Driving the third-generation 4WS was an entirely different ballgame. Honda states that the objective of four-wheel steering was to provide more control and stability during high-speed lane changes, in crowded parking lots or on icy roads. Indeed the 4WS did all of these things but at higher speeds steering response seemed slower than conventional-steering cars. Instead of the rear end sliding around the corner, it steers and essentially has to catch up.

Consider a radical maneuver in a two-wheel-steering car. The steered front tires must generate the force to rotate the car; the rear tires must not only rotate forward but also slide opposite of the turn. In a 4WS steering car under the same conditions, the rear tires begin making a cornering force almost immediately. The overall result is quicker response with less body roll.

At low speeds the rear tires turn opposite of the front which shortens the overall turning radius, allowing for tight maneuvers in parking lots. This got your attention immediately, especially in crowded traffic. Granted you could back into a spot in less space than you would have ever thought and making a U-turn was a breeze, but the first few corners were a bit unsettling.

The rear-steering wheels made the car feel as if it had a much shorter wheelbase. Once used to 4WS, you could take advantage of it in both low and high speed situations. The ultimate question was did it work? Absolutely. But was it the answer to the question nobody asked? The jury is still out, however *Road & Track*'s first test of the 4WS said that it can "move out of harms way where conventional cars may lose control." Gadget lovers undoubtedly pursued the 4WS for its uniqueness but it was not without a price tag.

You cannot beat the Prelude for touring. It felt equally as good on two-lane blacktop as on four-lane freeways. Performance was down just a tad from the previous year due to an increase in weight but only by a little. Making it perform was easy because pedal placement was perfect. There was even enough room for a legitimate heel-toe downshift!

Out of the box, the Prelude was still loaded with options but the price tag climbed over $20,000. The Si models were filled to the brim with every power option imaginable. The 1988 model added central door locking to the array and the moonroof was still in place.

All these standard features practically eliminated many aftermarket performance items but there were a few available. The majority of

What's wrong with these pictures? An excellent view of the Prelude's four-wheel steering. The 5.3 deg. of opposite steer looked and felt most obvious with the front wheels at full lock. The same steer at 1.5 deg. could barely be detected. Road & Track

parts available were primarily focused on the pre-1988 models. Tires, wheels and exhaust were about all you could change on the newer models. Tires were really not necessary as the Michelin MXVs handled just about anything well. Carburetor kits were available to replace the twin and single carb units and produced some noticeable power. There were also quite a few body accessories available including air dams, different rear spoilers and a full aero kit.

The Prelude finally attained the up-scale touring class Honda was aiming at when it debuted. The price tag might have climbed a bit high for Honda lovers who remember it as a $10,000 car but it had changed greatly since then. It is hard to imagine any improvements on the Prelude in its current form when you consider the Limited Edition, but you cannot help but wonder about its future with the introduction of the Accord Coupe.

The two cars were remarkably similar and sales on the Accord were booming. One might guess that a complete revision of the Prelude is in store—or it may evolve into a super sports car to compete with the real high-brow cars. Either way, if it is from Honda, it is sure to be good.

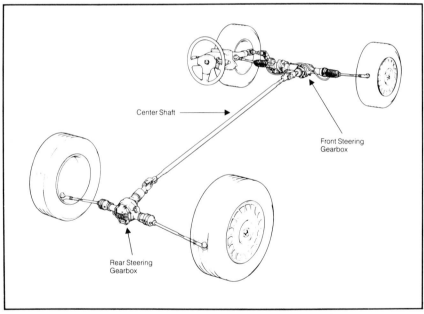

Center Shaft

Front Steering Gearbox

Rear Steering Gearbox

Honda's four-wheel steering was far less complex than it sounded. A simple shaft running the length of the car con- *nected the two steering boxes. Honda felt this system was far more reliable than an electric system.* Honda

Chapter 6

Legend, Sterling and Integra

Honda goes upscale

In 1986, Honda unveiled the Acura Automobile Division to the United States and brought out two new cars, the Integra and the Legend. The idea behind the new division and the new cars was to establish a line of upscale sports and luxury cars separate from the Honda name. The Legend was a four-door touring sedan aimed right at the heart of the luxury European market, while the Integra fell among the American and imported sports sedans.

Honda worked hard to make it clear the new line stood alone and even set up a separate dealer network. It seemed like a rather elaborate

When Honda unveiled its new line of upscale cars, it needed an upscale image for its dealerships. This was one of the plush new showrooms that could be found across the United States dur- *ing Acura's first two years. Bloomington Acura in Bloomington, Minnesota, was rated the number-one dealer among the original 240 Acura dealers.*

way of adding two new models to the line-up, yet in today's world of niche marketing, this strategy was not out of place. Sure, everyone knew the cars were made by Honda, but the different nameplate effectively cast a unique light on the cars. Oddly, Honda felt that only the American mar-

Honda's well-publicized entry bid into the high-performance sports car market. The Acura NS-X (New Sports Car-Experimental) features variable valve timing and a 3.0 liter V-6 with four camshafts and four valves per cylinder. The car is said to weigh less than 2,900 lb. and produce approximately 250 hp, which gives the NS-X a 0-to-60 mph time under 6 sec. and a top speed near 170 mph. Features include an all-aluminum version of the double-wishbone suspension, four-wheel vented disc brakes with anti-lock, traction control, a five-speed manual transmission and a luxurious leather-lined cockpit. The car is projected to cost in excess of $50,000 and should debut in 1990 with an initial production run of just 5,000 units.

There were many skeptics when Honda announced that it was building cars to compete with the world's upscale auto manufacturers. While the car was still a Honda, there was no doubt that the stately 1986 Acura Legend was a contender among luxury European cars.

The exotic-looking new Sterling 827SLi. The car is basically a hatchback version of the luxurious four-door model and features the programmed fuel-injected V-6 and four-wheel disc brakes.

ket needed this separation because in Europe and Japan the cars were known as Honda Integras and Honda Legends. Was it worth the effort? Hard to say, but big business is not the purpose of this book; cars are.

Legend and Sterling

Before we race off with the Integra, let's look at the Legend and its relative, the Sterling. By 1986, the Legend was the largest Honda built, measuring nearly 190 inches in length and weighing 3,100 lb. The car also featured Honda's largest engine: a 2500 cc twenty-four-valve V-6 that pumped out 151 hp at 5800 rpm.

Technically, the Legend had everything to offer that the high-ticket European cars did. This smooth and efficient powerplant could take you to 60 mph in 8.8 seconds. It had four-wheel disc brakes, front and rear anti-roll bars, rack-and-pinion steering and aggressive, fifteen-inch Michelin MXV 205/60 tires.

The Legend was able to compete in the comfort zone as well with a large roomy interior; electric windows, locks, mirrors and seats; climate-controlled heating and air conditioning; cruise control; tilt steering wheel; and an excellent radio and tape player. The dashboard presented a large speedometer and tachometer flanked by fuel and temperature gauges and controls at the fingertips. All this was standard and for a price in the mid-$20,000 range. Best of all, the car was designed and built by Honda, giving it that reputation of high reliability and low maintenance. This luxury sedan was even able to achieve EPA mileage ratings in the mid-twenties.

Cousin to the Legend was the British Sterling, a reskinned version of the same car. The Sterling's exterior was a little plainer than the Leg-

The luxurious Legend still said Honda when you sat behind the wheel. The dash layout was neat and simple with everything falling within fingertip reach. Acura did not offer an adjustable steering column in 1988 models because the car featured an airbag, and a tilted wheel may send the airbag in the wrong direction. Honda

One of the many fingertip convenience features of the Legend. Radio volume and station selection were easily within reach just beyond the right side of the wheel or on the radio.

The handy storage compartment on the Legend's dash. Again, Honda's convenience and storage theme carried over into the Acuras.

The Legend was designed to be plush and contend with world-class automobiles. Both the leather, shown here, and cloth seats were comfortable with plenty of support. Another Honda/ Acura convenience was the moving seatbelt arm at the base of the seat. It flipped toward the rear when the door was opened and forward when the door shut.

The automatic transmission in the Legend was fitted with the same sport-shift option found in the Preludes for 1988. This allowed the driver to change shift points to higher revs for quicker acceleration.

The rear seats in both the two- and four-door Legend were equally as plush and comfortable as the front. Plenty of leg and shoulder room made it easy for adults to ride in comfort. Notice the generous use of leather trim.

91

end's with flat fender sides and new grille and rear panel. The car was also English-ized on the inside with Connolly hides on the seats and a dashboard featuring burled walnut trim. As with the Legend, the Sterling came full-up with options but had a slightly higher price tag by about $5,000. A gimmick? Perhaps, but it was the first British car to offer the things synonymous with English cars, yet be free from the mechanical and electrical idiosyncrasies that trouble them.

The large, square center of the 1989 Legend's steering wheel may not be very attractive, but it does serve a purpose by housing the airbag.

The dash display in the Sterling is not that far removed from the Acura Legend. Controls are in the same places, but the Sterling's dash is more square while the Legend's is rounded. The major difference is the mahogany wood trim in front of the passenger, along the console and on the door panels.

Again, the similarities between the Legend and Sterling are very obvious, with the Sterling getting a much richer look. Note the wood trim along the top of the door. The Sterling also offers a fancier stereo with a separate tweeter positioned next to the door handle.

The Legend was quite a bit different from the Integra in both styling and market. Their sticker prices were separated by $10,000, and somehow the trunk on the Legend moved it above the hatch in the Integra. A true yuppie Honda at last!

Little changed on the Legend between its introduction and the 1988 model with the exception of color choices, anti-lock brakes and the optional air bag. You may have noticed that models equipped with the air bag do not come with an adjustable steering column. This was because Honda engineers were unsure of the air bag's performance with the wheel in positions other than the setting they deemed best.

Integra

When you first looked at the Integra, you might have thought that it would compete directly with cars like the Accord and Mazda 626. The Accord and Integra even looked similar, but they were very different cars. The Accord was a family-oriented car offering only a little performance, while the Integra was built for performance but offered plenty of room for the family. Perhaps the most interesting thing about the Integra was

The two-door Acura Integra in 1986, its inaugural year. It was originally billed as a luxury sports coupe, and it certainly lived up to the comfort level—the sportiness was left up to the eye of the buyer.

The 1986 debut four-door Integra.

that it was designed for the United States rather than starting off as a Japanese model, which would hopefully ensure a better fit in the US market.

The design did not connote sports car, perhaps not even sporty car, but once you got the Integra out on the road, you understood the basis for the claim to be a sports car. First, let's take a look at physical appearance.

The Integra came in either two-door or four-door form with your choice of the base RS trim or upscale LS trim. Measurements were simi-

The Integra's twin-cam powerplant was not only smooth and quick but nice to look at as well. The engine compartment was neatly laid out, with the exception of the washer fluid bottle. Only the cap was visible at the right side of the cam belt cover and the bottle hidden from view, leaving the driver to guess at the fluid level.

The other feature on the Special Edition was the rear spoiler. The word Special was fastened just below the right rear bumper.

Acura added a Special Edition to the Integra lineup. The Special Edition applied only to the three-door LS and came in either black with gold trim and gold wheels or white with white wheels. Both options had black and beige interiors. Standard equipment included a power moonroof, power windows, sport steering wheel and stiffer torsion bars. Only 5,000 were built in 1988.

lar to the four-door Civic design. The pattern of basic and upscale cars flowed into option selections as well.

Since these cars were Hondas, there was no question where the drive wheels were located. Both models were powered by a fuel-injected, sixteen-valve, dohc engine. This was the engine CRX lovers wished for, yet there were enough similarities so that you could almost have called the Integra a grown-up CRX.

The 1.6 liter powerplant produced 113 hp at 6250 rpm and 99 lb-ft of torque at 5500 rpm. That was enough to get from rest to the speed limit in just over nine seconds. Power-assisted disc brakes at all four corners brought the fourteen-inch Michelin MXVs back to rest easily.

The 1988 Integras got five more horsepower and a slight bump in torque via some changes in the fuel-injection brain box. Performance was about the same, but the increased torque allowed the car to pull much stronger through the rev band.

Suspension also mirrored that of the early CRXs with MacPherson struts, tube shocks and anti-roll bar in the front and beam axle with trailing arms, anti-roll bar, coil springs and tube shocks at the back. Power-assisted rack-and-pinion steering was also fitted to both editions as was the five-speed gearbox. A four-speed automatic could be ordered on all versions.

Ergonomics

Since all the running gear was the same, you only chose how you wanted your Integra wrapped. Both the RS and LS came right out of the box overflowing with enough standard features to make even a Prelude blush. The only exterior difference between the two was the wheels. The RS came with wheel covers, while the LS featured alloy wheels; these same rims were optional on the RS.

The Integra enhanced your driving enjoyment by giving you everything you could possibly want without asking. Personal preference for things like carpeting and a few power options helped you decide between

Softer, round switches replaced the rectangular switches in 1988. The designed location of the switches in the older and newer models is somewhat questionable since drivers may reach through the wheel rather than around it.

Buttons for electric locks and window lifts were located on the Integra's armrest, within easy reach. The driver could shut off the other window switches with the lock button and could lower his or her own window with one touch of the button rather than holding the button.

the RS and LS. Anything else could be ordered on the RS at an extra cost. Exclusive to the LS were power windows, power locks, fourteen-ounce carpet versus seven-ounce carpet on the RS, and cruise control. Only the three-door LS came with a sunroof.

Inside, everything was laid out neatly and logically. Looking past the adjustable steering column into the instrument pod revealed a large tachometer and a large speedometer in the center flanked by smaller temperature and fuel gauges. Wipers and lights were operated from large stalks on the sides of the wheel. Switches for the foglights and rear defoggers were found just below the information pod, which required you to reach around or through the wheel for access—perhaps not the wisest location. Your hands on the steering wheel at ten and two o'clock could obscure vision of the fuel and coolant gauges, but they are supplementary to the operation of the car.

The gauge pod was rearranged in the 1988 models, giving the driver three large dials to look into, rather than two large and two small as on the 1986 model. The switches below the pod were larger and more attractive as was the new four-spoke steering wheel.

Other changes for 1988 included a bit more support built into the front seats, new shoulder belts in the rear and latches to hook in child safety seats. A revised air dam was added out front, too.

The rest of the controls remained the same with heater and vent selectors sitting dead center on the dash and in easy reach of front-seat occupants. The now-standard pneumatic push buttons selected the mode, and a four-speed fan controlled the flow.

Once again, Honda/Acura gave you a choice of radios, installed at the dealer, ranging from a basic AM/FM radio to three styles of AM/FM cassette players and an optional graphic equalizer. The radio-powered four speakers mounted in the front doors and above the rear shock towers. Here again were two options: basic dual cones or co-axial speakers. True audiophiles could also select a compact disc player with the 1988 models.

The size of the Integra offers you a wide variety of aftermarket sound systems if you don't like Honda's. Do-it-yourselfers can easily install a radio and speakers since all the wiring has been done for you. Simply purchase the plug-in adaptor, and you are in business. The rear speaker holes do not offer the capacity for larger, more powerful speakers, and some cutting may be necessary.

The folks at Honda have realized the potential extras and offer a catalog of all sorts of goodies you can buy directly from the dealer. These include basic mudflaps and floor mats plus car covers, rear-window louvers, leather steering wheel, nose masks and even Acura apparel. If you are contemplating any add-ons, the catalog is a good place to start shopping since the merchandise is all made specifically for the Integra and will fit correctly. Another nice extra is the Acura owners magazine published quarterly for Integra and Legend drivers. The magazine is a glitzy, color piece with articles about Acura cars and lifestyle features.

Overall fit and finish in the Integra was excellent. The only problem seems to be that the glovebox door never quite lined up. Door panel inserts and seats were covered in a plush, velourlike fabric giving a rich appearance. It is too early to tell how well the cloth will wear.

Both front and rear seats were comfortable, and driving position was excellent. You sat up much higher in the Integra than in other Honda automobiles. This gave you excellent visibility, especially out over the low hood. The seats provided excellent support, and the side bolsters were not obtrusive or too stiff. They were sure to hold you snugly during fast driving and were comfortable for the long haul.

Unlike other Honda automobiles, the Integra offered plenty of room in the back for two or three adults to ride comfortably, even in the two-door. The split rear seat also folded down to give you extra cargo space. The rear shelf was actually a removable cargo cover that flipped open from inside the car or from outside when the hatch was open. There was ample luggage space for two or three people when the seats were in the up position, but additional cargo required some careful planning.

Driving

Whether it was those tedious trips across town or getting lost on a twisting country road, the Integra made them all a pleasure. The Integra

Seats in the Integra were form-fitting with good lateral support and leg support. The cloth material matched the interior trim. Shown are seats from the Special Edition, which only came in black with tan inserts.

Both two- and four-door Integra models featured rear cargo covers to keep belongings out of sight. The cover flipped up in both directions, allowing access through the rear hatch or from the rear seat. It was also completely removable for carrying larger items.

The rear of the Integra with the cargo cover removed. The split, folding rear seats left plenty of room for carrying passengers and large parcels.

was easily Honda's best-mannered road car. The twin-cam engine responded to even the lightest touch and pulled hard all the way to the 7000 rpm redline if you hoofed it hard. The rev limit came up quickly once you hit the power band at about 3500 rpm and the engine practically sang all the way there. Maximum horsepower and torque were delivered at rather high rpm since most four-valve engines require more flow to realize peak power, making it all the more fun to wind it up.

Cruising was smooth and quiet in the Integra. At 60 mph you heard only a little hum as the twin-cam whirred at just under 3000 rpm, and the flush-mount windows and aerodynamic skin brought wind noise to a minimum.

As always, the engine was paired with a silky smooth, five-speed transmission. Shifts were short and crisp, and the clutch had just the right amount of firmness. Pedal placement was also well-designed and easily aligned for proper heel-toe action. Neither the brakes nor accelerator required much effort or absolute precision, allowing even the novice the ability to master Andretti-like up-and-down shifts through the corners. The 9.5 inch front discs and 9.4 inch rear discs stopped the car better than the same equipment in many high-priced European cars and within a couple of feet of cars equipped with ABS.

ABS, or anti-lock brake system, is a computer-controlled braking system that keeps even stopping power on all four wheels without allowing the car to lock up or skid. This gives the driver better control in a panic stop and brings the car to rest in a shorter distance than do conventional brakes.

The owners manual told you to take it easy on the brakes during the break-in period. This was because the discs were a softer metal and could warp from heavy stress and heat. Honda meant it too.

The platform of the Integra offered excellent characteristics for racing. This is the tube-frame Integra built by King Honda of Milwaukee, Wisconsin.

Shiftless operators were right at home with the four-speed automatic. It shifted smoothly and quietly although a few problems affected the automatic gearbox and it could not stand up to abuse, especially when changing from forward to reverse or vice versa while the car was still in motion. This resulted in the gearbox becoming sloppy and in hard shifting. The cars came with a warning tag on the shift lever which meant the problem still had not been solved.

Maneuvering the Integra was easy with the power-assisted steering, although it was perhaps a little too light. Steering was effortless in daily driving through town and parking lots, but a little more feel would have been nice when cornering hard.

As with all Honda products, understeer was the name of the game, and the Integra was no exception. This understeer was not as excessive as in other Honda cars, however, and you didn't find yourself getting in trouble as often as you could in a CRX.

Tires didn't seem to be as much the culprit here either. The Michelin MXVs did an admirable job of gripping the road although something stickier enhanced cornering quite a bit.

Body roll in the Integra was not as obvious as in other Hondas either. Perhaps this was due to its being a larger car and having slightly stiffer suspension. One characteristic that grabbed your attention was the lift-throttle, or trailing-throttle, oversteer. Backing off the power in a corner caused enough of a weight transfer that the rear end seemingly floated toward the outside of the corner. This was solved with a little practice in tempering your touch on the accelerator as you went through corners.

Insurance

The only other little irritation you may have encountered with the Integra was insurance. The words twin-cam lit up the insurance agent's eyes as do big cubic inches and sports cars. The three-door cost more to insure than the five-door, and the rate varied depending on your age, geographic location and driving record. City dwellers came to expect premiums approaching $1,000 per year for full coverage. Rural folks only saved a few hundred dollars.

Shop long and hard to find your best price.

Maintenance

Honda/Acura has tried to cover all the bases with the Integra, and the effort shows. This is the most refined car the company has yet produced, and few things could improve it.

The plastic steering wheel and shift knob detract from the sportiness of the car. Acura offers an optional leather wheel, but you will have to shop elsewhere for the shift knob.

Although the dashboard was revised for 1988, the fuel gauge was a problem. You no doubt discovered quite a bit of gas remained in the tank—about three gallons—even though the needle indicated empty. You can do little but keep track of mileage. Under normal driving conditions, you should get nearly 400 miles per tankful.

Another frustrating item was found, or not found, under the hood. The windshield washer reservoir was so buried that you could not determine how much was in the jug without topping it off. This may sound trivial, but many people have to rely on the washer fluid during the slushy seasons.

An additional problem was a faulty switch that caused the panel lights to flicker, but the dealer should gladly take care of it for you. These were small bumps in the highway of life and hardly damning to the Integra.

Summary

The Integra has only been around for a few years so its durability cannot be judged yet. Given Honda's reputation for quality, it is hard to envision any big problems. One question has been answered: Can a family-looking sedan be sporty and fun? The answer is a resounding yes.

Changes are hard to predict for the Integra. As of 1988, the car had not changed dramatically since its introduction in 1986, which means a new Integra may be just over the horizon. Most obvious would be a changeover to the double wishbone suspension prevalent in the new Honda line. This would mean new body panels because the double wishbones allow for a lower hoodline.

Chapter 7

Fast driving

Now that you know the Hondas and Acuras inside, outside and underneath, let's look at the real reason you bought one—the fun. How many times have you caught yourself smiling as you zip through traffic in town or zoom down a winding country road? The CRX loves to do either. No numerical rating measures this pleasure, but most CRX road tests practically guarantee you fun.

Front-drive versus rear-drive

Before we go charging into our first corner, let's look at the basic elements of driving because you need to understand some important principles. Consider the three basic things you do in a car: steer, brake and accelerate. Now think about a corner and what you expect the front tires to do: they must absorb the majority of the braking pressure, they must turn and, in a front-drive car, they must also accelerate out of the corner.

The overwhelming factor that affects how you steer, brake and accelerate is the weight distribution in a front-wheel-drive car: nearly all the weight is biased toward the front—and under braking the shift is even greater yet. In a rear-drive car most of the braking is done by the front

The King Honda tube-frame Integra at speed on the Atlanta racetrack.

101

wheels, yet in a front-drive car it is even greater. Obviously, it is good to have a high degree of downforce, or loading, on the front wheels because downforce delivers greater traction, which means you can turn better. In theory this is correct, but in practice there are too many variables. Yes, more downforce is better, but only up to a point.

These variables are tires, suspension and driver. Yes, you. Ask yourself if you are giving the car what it needs during a corner or are you trying to make it do what you expect? What you expect is usually based on previous experience in a rear-drive car. The front-drive car is different.

It is easy to overload the front tires. Braking hard puts tremendous pressure on the front, turning into the corner adds even more force up front and the outside front tire takes nearly all of the cornering load. What happens? You continue to turn the wheel, but the car goes where the nose is pointed, not where the wheels are pointed. This is understeer and every front-drive does it.

The two biggest factors in understeer are tires and driver input. If the tires are too small and/or not sticky enough, you are going to reach or

The versatility of the CRX allows it to be driven to the track, and a quick change to studded tires makes a street- *stock CRX Si into a fiery competitor. Here, a 1987 Si powers around a turn in a Midwest ice racing event.*

The layout and power-to-weight ratio in the CRX have made it an excellent racecar for a variety of racing styles. *Here, an early CRX powers up a mountain course in a road rally event.* Jackson Racing

102

exceed the tires' limit of performance almost immediately. Once you have reached this point, the front tires will begin to slide sideways rather than track or turn.

Giving the car power unloads the front tires and transfers the weight/force to the rear, but too much power can underload the front tires to the point where they will also slip. I am sure you have sensed this because at this point you hear the revs climb quickly and you can turn the wheel easily all the way to lock, yet nothing happens. The car is revving because the outboard tire is overloaded and the inside front is underloaded from body roll and so the tire is spinning.

This is where driver sensitivity takes over. Assessment of the problem is difficult since the power-assisted steering does not give you a good feel for slip angle. However, steering is not the factor here.

Cornering

Cornering in the CRX was a scream. You may have screamed the first time you really charged into a corner and discovered the surprising amount of bodyroll and understeer in the car. Overall bodyroll was actually small but appeared more pronounced due to the short wheelbase.

The long sweeping corners are the most fun in a CRX. Now that we have learned some of the dynamics of cornering loads and braking, you can see why. A firm but gentle squeeze of the accelerator will carry you through the curve with ever increasing speeds. In fact, you are more than likely to have a higher exit speed than a rear-drive car because the bodyroll is already putting downforce on the front tires giving you more traction. A rear-drive car will tend to oversteer, and the driver will have to come off the power to keep the car on the road.

Conversely, the tight corners favor the rear-drive car. They can oversteer into position, apply power and go. These corners require the front-drive car to brake, turn and accelerate with heavy loads on the drive wheels. The key here is to brake later and keep on the brakes until the apex, keeping the front wheels loaded, then make the gentle transition to power. The problem is that experience tells you to brake early and then you are ready to go back to the gas before the car is ready. This causes power-understeer where the inside wheel is spinning, you have a tremen-

Prior to the days of double-wishbone suspension, a 1987 CRX exhibits some obvious bodyroll. The inside tires have *become unloaded, and the car swings into an understeer stance.*

103

dous slip angle and you lower your exit speed. The other advantage to staying on the brakes longer is that your foot is already on the pedal that will help bail you out of trouble.

Your instant reaction is to steer out of the situation because that is what the rear-drive car taught you, but it is your foot that is causing the problem. Excessive braking or power is the reason for the steering deficiency, so you should ease off on either the brake or the gas enough to allow the front wheels back within their limit of performance.

Once you were comfortable with the rolling effect, you could be prepared for it and negotiate even the sharpest corners. I found that the long sweepers are more fun than the left-right switchbacks because you don't get tossed back and forth by the body roll.

It was critical that you came off the throttle gradually. Never snap off the throttle during a corner unless it is absolutely necessary. Snapping out of the power during a fast corner would bring the back end around faster than you could say trailing-throttle-oversteer. Your only recourse at this point was to throw in the clutch, stab the brakes, close your eyes and hang on until it was all over. The light throttle action was a boon in this situation as you could easily breathe out of the power without getting into trouble.

The principles of tire loading and cornering held true for the newest version of the CRX; especially with the boost in power. Accelerating hard out of a corner would produce wheelspin from the inside wheel. With experience and the proper steering and throttle inputs you could control all these things.

Tires

A lot of the handling quirks resulted from tires. Honda gave you all the performance and sophistication you could ask for but for some reason skimped on the rubber. The Yokohama AX 323s were a bit too hard a compound for the CRX's abilities, and something fatter and stickier like 001 or 008 Yokohamas or Bridgestone RE71s improved performance vastly.

A simple upgrade in tires made all the difference in the world. You may have even asked yourself how you got along with the original set. The models mentioned above are definitely high-line tires that can carry a hefty price tag. Don't fool around with inexpensive tires; they are all you have between you and the road.

Remembering the rear-drive analogy, think about where the largest tires are mounted on a racing car—on the drive wheels. The same holds true for front-drive; more tire on the wheels doing all the work will give you more grip under power and braking. Ideally, you would also want smaller tires on the rear to reduce their grip so the back begins to come around, thereby reducing understeer. But this is not usually done on front-drive cars because it looks silly to have large tires in the front and little ones in the back.

Chassis and suspension

The CRX chassis was an excellent design. It was loaded with all sorts of engineering refinements, but a few quirks became apparent when you put it through its paces. Steering was light and effortless in all three models, and I have already addressed the differences in steering ratios between the HF and the base CRX.

The 1988 Si got variable-rate power-assisted steering for improved response and handling. The Si did indeed have a slightly heftier grip and gave an even stronger sense of grip at speed. Lower speeds and parking required a little more energetic handling of the steering wheel as there was quite a bit more resistance when the car was not rolling.

The new suspension design in the 1988 models had many benefits. With the demise of the rigid rear axle, the thumping from bumps and expansion joints no longer echoed in the cargo area.

The pre-1988 models did not use the later double wishbone suspension, and had definite understeer but not excessive—in fact it was predictable. When running hard, you could toss the car into a corner and have it do all those nasty understeer things associated with a front-drive car and have it plowing toward the outside. However, the nimble steering and the short wheelbase made it a breeze to master the CRX.

In an early road test *Road & Track* said "understeer develops early and grows to enormous proportions at maximum lateral acceleration." Obviously this was done as a test but I have experienced a similar situation while attempting to accelerate hard through a clover leaf. The CRX's handling can be summed up in a follow-up *Road & Track* road test: "Dial in predictable front-drive understeer and you have a demon handler that will out corner a good many so-called 'road cars.' "

The new version with the double-wishbones had much more precise steering with what *Motor Trend* called "throw-it-anywhere agility." The new suspension kept the car relatively flat and with only mild understeer, thus making it mostly neutral in handling. Some inexperienced drivers might have gotten themselves in a bit of trouble with the quick steering. *Car and Driver* said, "The steering is micro-meter accurate; in most situations the CRX shadows your moves." This could have been a

Four-Wheel
Double Wishbone
Suspension

A cutaway view of the 1988 double-wishbone suspension for the CRX. This was the same layout used in the Accord and Prelude. The suspension takes up little space and allows for a much lower and more aerodynamic body shape.

problem if you made the wrong determination about what was going to take place.

The new suspension in the 1988 models nearly eliminated all understeer tendencies, and the car was surprisingly neutral even though the bodyroll still prevailed. The new model had only a slight understeer when charging through a corner, and taking your foot off the loud pedal gave you only a slight oversteer. With practice you could balance the two nicely: back off on the power when you started to get into trouble, bring the car back to neutral and carry on.

The new models tended to have less nosedive under hard braking. The dive was not nearly as pronounced as in the original Civics which would practically stand on the front bumper when you pounced on the brakes. The 1988s dipped ever so slightly and maintained excellent control with minimal fade even after a thorough stomping. The earlier models would occasionally lock the rear brakes sooner than you wanted because the rear end was so severely unloaded, but that seemed to have been remedied in the 1988 edition.

There was minimal torque-steer for a front-drive car with such formidable power. Honda was able to achieve this minimal level with equal-length driveshafts which have different diameters. Unfortunately, the cars suffered from a fair amount of bump-steer, especially when starting out. Wheel travel was good, but the suspension could still be pretty rough on you and make some rather awful noises.

The brakes were able to bring the CRX to a halt from 60 mph in 141 feet, which nipped the previous model's performance by three feet. Imagine what the four-wheel discs could do!

Throttle control

The feather-light throttle action was a boon to the CRX in all corner situations. It was easy to squeeze on or gently let off the gas to control the corner. Come off it just right and you could bring on some oversteer to straighten out the corner and reduce front tire scrubbing.

The car never tires of racing up to redline. You have probably noticed, however, that the red zone comes up quickly once you hit the power band. In the pre-1988 models, the lights came on right around 3500 rpm, and the car pulled hard all the way to the 6500 rpm cap. On the other hand, the 1988 CRX pulled strong right off the line but faded a bit in the top of the rev band; this was due to gearing. The 1988 would have benefited from a little taller first gear so you wouldn't have to change so soon after getting moving. You may have also found that during occasional quick shifts in the earliest models you are able to beat the synchros and chomp the gears a bit. Your best remedy here is simply to take it a little easier.

Summary

Overall, the CRX is an excellent, well-mannered road car that loves to go out to play any time you want to. You can cruise for hours, and no matter how much you flog it, there is no way you can get poor gas mileage. The cars are as cool and calm on the interstate highways as they are on two-laners, with effortless steering and a feather touch on the accelerator.

The 1988 CRX has already proved a worthy competitor on road courses across the United States. King Motorsports of Milwaukee, Wisconsin has built the first-ever tube-frame CRX racing car. The car was completely fabricated from scratch to meet the exact dimensions of a stock CRX. Before the first race date, a fiberglass body will be fitted.

107

Chapter 8

Aftermarket accessories

Thousands of CRXs zoom around the countryside. You see them every day; you probably have even gotten the approving nod from other CRX drivers when you encounter them in traffic. Yet, because the cars are all similar, many drivers are looking for ways to personalize their CRXs and make them a little different.

In answer to this quest, a plethora of aftermarket companies offer a variety of performance and appearance products for the CRX. Some companies have done their homework and offer you items that truly benefit your car, while others are just capitalizing on the popularity of the car. The two biggest players are Mugen and Jackson Racing. Their cars have been featured on the covers of a number of the leading automotive magazines over the years. Both Jackson and Mugen have extensive catalogs of

For those of you who are just proud to drive the car, Acura offers a host of apparel and cosmetic items. This ranges from shirts and sweaters to pens and coffee mugs. They are available through Acura dealers and the Acura magazine.

accessories with many recommendations, yet when it comes down to decision time, only you can be the judge of what is right for you and your car. However, I will touch on a few considerations.

Cosmetic changes

The quickest, easiest and most noticeable change you can make is cosmetic. All kinds of parts are available that can make subtle or outrageous changes to the appearance of your car. These consist of spoilers, air dams and skirts. They may look simple to install and some are, but make sure you can handle the job before drilling holes in your car. You can also add anything from pinstripes to tinted windows to louvers. All are readily available from your local parts shop and even your Honda dealer.

Any of these things will make an instant change in the appearance of your car. Other subtle but individualistic changes include steering wheels, shift knobs and seats. What a difference a steering wheel can make. This little change can give you a completely new outlook on your Honda and even affect how you drive. Consider this: all the time you spend in your Honda you have to sit in the same seat, hold the same steering wheel and use the same shift knob over and over again. Why not be comfortable?

Performance upgrades are as important and individual as they are nonvisual. You cannot see a new camshaft or new shocks, and tires are always black and round, but oh, do they make a difference.

There are many wheels available from a variety of aftermarket dealers, but check your Honda dealer first. Honda offers a nice selection of custom wheels to accent your car, whether it be a Civic, Accord, Prelude or CRX. Remember that correct offset is critical, and you can be certain these wheels will fit.

Tires and wheels

When contemplating performance upgrades for your car, tires unquestionably are the first and foremost consideration. The original tires Honda put on the car are good enough for daily driving and some mildly spirited driving, but a simple upgrade can make a world of difference.

Your first inclination is probably to go to fatter rubber. Sure, the car will look much tougher and more aggressive, but you may be hindering performance rather than enhancing it. You shouldn't go any larger than a 175/70-13 or a 185/60-14 tire. Anything larger will throw your handling way off because the entire tire will not get up to the proper temperature for optimum adhesion and you could end up with less grip than with the original tires. Bigger tires will also confuse your speedometer and beat the heck out of your fenderwells from rubbing. Too large a tire can also cause excess bearing wear.

Don't go out and buy a fancy high-performance tire just because of the name and the price tag. A number of square-shouldered tires like the Goodyear Gatorback and Pirelli P6 and P7 deliver optimum performance on rear-wheel-drive cars. They are excellent tires, and they will work better than your originals, but you have a front-drive car that can benefit even more from a different tire.

Rubber compound and tread pattern should be your concerns when making out your shopping list. You want a fairly soft, sticky compound that is also good in the wet. Yes, a soft compound means you will have to replace the tires sooner than usual, but if you want serious performance you need serious tires.

Jackson Racing has done some thorough tire testing; they have gotten the best results with the Yokohama AVS, A001R and super-sticky A008R as well as the Bridgestone RE71 and Fulda 2000. I've also found a

Here are just a couple of examples of wheels available from other sources. Both the Momo and Aries wheels are available from a number of dealers including Jackson Racing, and they will fit the CRX, Accord and Prelude. These wheels are designed for proper fit and hubcentricity to eliminate vibration. The look and cost of these wheels call for a wheel locking kit if you want to sleep at night. Jackson Racing

good intermediate tire in the Falken FX06C. Whatever you decide, shop thoroughly and remember, performance has a price tag.

Now, what to mount your new tires on? You want something that looks hot and accents the car well. Before you rush down to your local speed show, check with your Honda dealer first. Honda offers some good-looking wheels that rival some aftermarket models—and you know they will fit properly. If Honda's wheels don't grease your gears, some great wheels are available from a variety of sources. Remember that offset, bolt pattern and hub center are crucial to proper performance. The wrong combination will cause vibrations and could harm the suspension. Make sure the wheels you are considering are hubcentric to Hondas and not a one-size-fits-all. If the wheel is not correct, you will get vibrations above 60 mph.

My only personal reservation is that you do not put whitewall tires on your Honda. The car was not designed to have them, and they look awful.

Suspension

Keeping with the performance theme, your next consideration is suspension components. A number of companies offer stiffer springs, shocks and anti-roll bars. You cannot buy a perfect kit or perfect parts; you simply make changes that make you comfortable. Some people like a stiffer ride than others, and some like the CRX just the way it is. The folks at Mugen feel that your original-equipment shocks are more or less used up by the 15,000 mile point. Both Mugen and Jackson racing recommend the firm strut with coil spring for the best results, although Jackson also carries gas shocks for those who are sold on the concept.

To me, the most beneficial addition would be stiffer anti-roll bars at both ends to cut down on body roll. It will decrease the load on the front tires during cornering and allow you to be quicker through the turns. Be

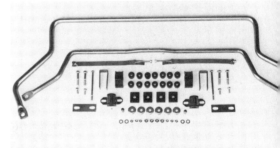

Your CRX handles well, but you can flatten out those corners even more with these two kits from Jackson Racing. The Tokico gas strut and spring assembly bolts in directly and easily, *while the suspension kit takes more time and know-how. The average home mechanic should plan on a weekend project.* Jackson Racing

sure that the one you purchase is made of spring steel; anything else is below the manufacturer's standards and could break prematurely.

Engine

Beyond wheels, tires and suspension, the rest is completely up to the individual's preference. If ultimate performance is your goal, nearly all Honda specialists offer cams, cranks, pistons, carburetors, headers and the like. Several companies even offer turbo systems for the CRX. Just to dazzle you with a few numbers, the Jackson Racing Turbo kit pushes horsepower to 166 and the Cartech system rates a couple of horses higher. Both are working on systems for the 1988 models.

If you are going to do the work, be sure you know what you're getting into and ask the supplier what is involved. Most have information lines just for this purpose. Keep in mind that many of these modifications will void your new car warranty, so if you install something incorrectly and your motor has itself for lunch, don't go complaining to your Honda garage.

If your tastes and skills are limited to something less kinky than cams, cranks and turbos, you can do some simple bolt-ons in an afternoon

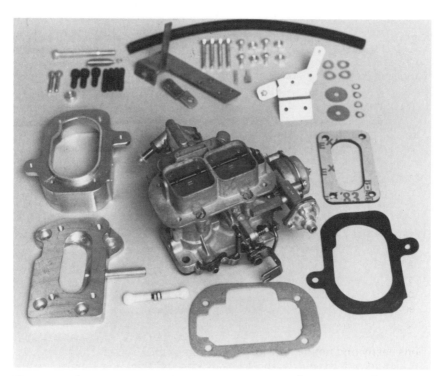

You can realize an instant and noticeable power increase by letting your Honda breathe more freely. This is a typical Weber conversion kit that can be installed in an afternoon. The unit is preset so there are no adjustments. The Weber delivers quicker throttle response and, in many cases, even better mileage. Jackson Racing

with basic mechanical knowledge. These include mufflers, distributors, carbs and ignition sets. All will give you a slight boost in performance.

Mugen

The proper pronunciation is moo-gan, and it means "unlimited." The Japan-based company engineers and manufactures aftermarket upgrades for Hondas and Acuras.

Mugen was founded in 1973 by Hirotoshi Honda, son of Soichiro Honda, founder of Honda Motor, and is run as a separate and independent company. It has been heavily involved with the CRX since its introduction—in fact, a Mugen-ized CRX was displayed at the 1983 CRX unveiling in Japan.

The company's first project was building a Formula FJ engine from the 1200 cc Civic engine. Mugen either modified or completely remade everything on the engine right down to the oil pan. The engine was bored out to 1273 cc and fed by four 35 mm Keihin carburetors and produced 135 hp. Mugen won its first race with the engine and within three years won the championship.

Today Mugen is building racing engines and components for go-karts, motocross motorcycles, Formula Three, Formula Two, SCCA GT-4, and IMSA CRXs and Integras. Most notable is that Mugen was the force behind the dominance of the McLaren-Honda's world championship for the 1988 Grand Prix season.

American Honda Motor Company and Mugen were originally going to team up and offer competition parts designed and tested by Mugen through Honda dealers across the country. The dealer distribution program fell through, and Mugen parts are now available through King Motorsports, a division of King Honda, in Milwaukee, Wisconsin.

Mugen selected the midwestern Honda dealer to be its authorized parts distributor because of King's racing history. President Jim Dentici grabbed the limelight in SCCA GT-4 racing when he entered a race-prepped Civic in 1981. After many lap records and victories, Dentici drove a Honda to the national championship in 1984. In 1985, King Motorsports built the first Honda to compete in the IMSA Radial Sedan series. Since that time, Dentici's Hondas have consistently finished in the top five. Today, that original 1981 Civic is still competing in GT-4 competition.

The philosophy behind Mugen equipment is that it is engineered specifically for Honda and Acura cars as they work closely with Honda Motor Company. All of Mugen's components are track-tested at Honda's proving grounds in Japan and at the Suzuka racetrack to ensure they meet the high standards expected by Honda. The result is top-quality components that fit precisely and use original bolts, brackets and hangers whenever possible. This allows the do-it-yourselfer to make modifications easily and not have to jury-rig things or make special adjustments.

Mugen offers wheels, shocks, body kits, soft trim items and an extensive selection of engine components including headers, pistons, cams, engine blocks, heads, limited-slip differentials, exhaust systems and even a close-ratio gearbox. It is interesting to note that the man who makes the Mugen aftermarket header assembly is the same man making the header system for Ayrton Senna's world champion Formula One car.

The first improvement Mugen recommends is flattening out the cornering with some stiffer anti-roll bars. This reduces cornering loads substantially and makes the car more responsive. The rear anti-roll bar for the CRX and Integra fits inside the rear tube-axle and can be installed easily. The front anti-roll bar fits directly in place of the original bar and uses the same mounting points and hardware. Some anti-roll bars are added on to the existing unit rather than replacing it altogether. Mugen warns that adding an anti-roll bar in this fashion can do more harm than good because they are not meant to work together.

Mugen also offers several complete suspension kits with struts, springs, anti-roll bars and torque tubes. Each setup was originally designed from the Group A racing Hondas in Japan and match exactly.

To get the most bang-for-your-buck, try the Mugen exhaust system. It is a complete front-to-rear system including header, pipes and muffler with chrome-tipped tailpipe. Naturally, it is designed to use the original mounting brackets. Not only will you instantly notice the deeper, throaty tone, but the free-breathing exhaust boosts horsepower.

Mugen also offers an array of internal engine components including valves and valve springs, camshafts, high-compression pistons and more. All this equipment is precise and high-quality; everything has a purpose and a direct benefit. Take for example the oil pan set for the Integra. This simple change can add five horsepower to the car's performance.

The CRX and Integra are the primary beneficiaries of Mugen's efforts. However, a number of parts are available for the Prelude and older Civics.

Jackson Racing

Like most aftermarket operations, Jackson Racing is located in Southern California, specifically Huntington Beach. The company was founded in 1979 by Oscar Jackson who first got hooked up with Honda when racing motorcycles in 1968. Shortly afterward, he was shop foreman at a major California Honda automobile dealership until he went into business for himself.

Jackson's operation is divided in two sections, sales and service. The service division not only offers conventional repairs on Honda automobiles but also high-performance engine and chassis building. The sales division offers Honda and Acura owners high-performance components and many accessory items via their mail-order catalog.

Many of Jackson Racing's parts are designed and race-tested by Oscar Jackson himself, driver Lance Stewart and chief mechanic Marc Grunfor. Some of Jackson's titles include 1986 SSB National Championship in a CRX Si, 1986 Pro Solo National Championship D3 in a 1986 Si, 1986 Solo II National Championship GSL in an Acura Integra, 1984 Solo II National Championship in a CRX and the Group B, class A-9 World Rally event in the 1986 Olympus Rally in a Jackson-prepared CRX Si.

Jackson Racing's catalog boasts a large selection of parts and accessories for Hondas and Acuras, including the Civic, Prelude, Accord, CRX, Integra and even the Legend. Just about everything is pictured with an honest description of what it will do for your car. It will also tell you how to do the project and estimate the time needed to complete it.

Everything is available to build a street sleeper as long as you have the original car, the time and of course, the money. The 1988 CRX is an all-new model, yet Jackson Racing has approximately 20,000 test miles on the car already and a host of items available for it including springs, shocks, anti-roll bars, adjustable camber kits, headers, mufflers, cams, pistons, body kits, wheels and tires.

So what does the team at Jackson Racing recommend you do to your Honda or Acura? First and foremost, they suggest a tire upgrade. The tires that come on the car are fine for getting groceries, but they are not designed for performance driving. Jackson's first choice for a long-lasting high-performance tire that delivers good traction and handling is the Yokohama AVS. It is a good intermediate tire and should last approximately 35,000 miles. The fastest tire is the Yokohama A008R, but since it is a softer compound it will not last nearly as long.

The next step is to tune-up the suspension. Jackson Racing offers several kits, but their most popular is what they call the Road Atlanta kit. The kit is tops in their three-stage suspension upgrade and consists of front and rear stabilizer bars, bushings, coil sport springs and Tokico gas shocks. People who know their way around a car should be able to install it in three to four hours. The results will be much flatter cornering, improved transitional response and resistance to bottoming out, and it will cut down on inside wheel lift.

These two modifications alone will make a marked difference in the Honda you drive every day. Beyond that, the enhancements you want are made at your discretion. Obviously, after you've upgraded the twists and turns, the next bit is power. Jackson offers enough go-fast goodies to push CRX horsepower over 130 and for far less money than you'd think.

If your objective is to get noticed, there are also spoilers, air dams, body kits, steering wheels, seats and shift knobs—it depends on your taste. Some automotive journals have lauded Jackson's CRX as a giant-killer, but you have to admit the 1.6 liter engine is somewhat limiting—or is it?

Cartech

Cartech of Dallas, Texas, has developed an intercooled turbocharger for the CRX that can throw stones at many of the Goliaths. Cartech boasts a dyno-test 160 hp and allows for the use of the factory fuel and emissions systems. The 200 piece system offers an optional water-cooled turbo bearing with in-car boost control with a predetermined low and high setting. You can tackle the kit yourself if you have a good working knowledge of what goes on under the hood, or you can have Cartech install it for a fee. Obviously, such a kit will cost far more than the bolt-on goodies from Jackson.

If you love power, acceleration and torque, you will enjoy Cartech's system. Boost comes in at 1800 rpm and pulls hard toward redline. Because it spins so quickly, you might want to opt for the redline warning buzzer or rev limiter. For bench racers, this translates into 0 to 60 mph in approximately six seconds and a quarter-mile in the low fourteen-second range. That's enough to frustrate a lot of high-horsepower drivers. Naturally, all this power cannot be harnessed by the stock rubber so you will need to upgrade to something a little more sticky. The turbo will also have some effect on the engine, increasing wear by ten percent; fuel economy will also suffer by about ten percent. A turbo system for the Integra is still under consideration.

If you want to dress it up at the same time you boost it up, Cartech also offers wheels, tires and body kits.

Pure power is what the Cartech turbo system is all about. This intercooled system can boost the CRX's horsepower output to around 160 hp. The unit features in-car boost control and a water-cooled bearing. Obviously not a project for the faint-hearted; Cartech suggests a good mechanic can complete the installation in thirty hours. Cartech

Sources

Jackson Racing
16291 Gothard St.
Huntington Beach, CA 92693

AT Engineering
2 Candlewood Rd.
Milford, CT 06776

Dobi
320-C Thor Pl.
Brea, CA 92621

Beverly Hills Motoring Accessories
200 South Robertson Blvd.
Beverly Hills, CA 90211

Cartech
11212 Goodnight Ln.
Dallas, TX 75229

Mugen
King Motorsports
4585 South 76th
Milwaukee, WI 53220

RC Engineering
1728 Border Ave.
Torrance, CA 90501

Shankle Automotive
9135-F Alabama Ave.
Chatsworth, CA 91311

Reliable Motoring Accessories
1751 Spruce St.
Riverside, CA 92507

S800 coupe.

N500.

S Series 1962–68
S360, S500, S600, S800
Engine type
354 cc on S360
531 cc on S500
606 cc on S600
791 cc on S800
Water-cooled
Four cylinder
Double overhead camshaft
Roller bearing crankshaft
Transmission
Four-speed manual
Brakes
1962–66: Front drum, rear drum
1966–68: Front disk, rear drum
Suspension
Front: Independent with torsion bar
and hydraulic damper
Rear 1962–66: Independent with
chain drive
Rear 1966–68: Live axle, independent
with radius rod, coil spring, hydraulic damper
Body style
Two-door convertible
Two-door coupe
Dimensions
Length: 131 in.
Width: 55 in.
Height: 47.8 in. (top up)
Instruments
Speedometer
Tachometer
Fuel
Water

N Series 1966–72
N360, N400, N500, N600, 600 coupe
Engine type
354 cc on N360
401 cc on N400
500 cc on N500
598 cc on N600 and 600 coupe
Air-cooled*
Two cylinder
Single overhead camshaft
Transmission
Four-speed manual
Three-speed Hondamatic, introduced
1968
Brakes
Power-assisted front disk
Rear drum
Suspension
Front: Independent coil springs
Rear: Semi-elliptic leaf springs
Steering
Rack and pinion
Body style
Two-door sedan
Two-door coupe with rear hatch
Dimensions
Length: 118 in.; 122 in. N600
Width: 51 in.
Height: 50 in.
Instruments
Coupe: Speedometer
Tachometer
Fuel
Sedan: Speedometer
Fuel

*Aircooling aided by axial flow fan
located behind the engine, supplemented by ram air.

118

First-generation Civic hatchback.

First-generation Civic wagon.

Civic, first generation 1973–79
1200, 1300, 1500
Engine type
1973–74: 1200 cc
Water-cooled
Four cylinder
Single overhead camshaft
1975–79: 1300 cc and 1500 cc
Water-cooled
Four cylinder
Single overhead camshaft
CVCC
Transmission
Four-speed manual
Three-speed Hondamatic
Five-speed manual 1975
Brakes
Front disk

Rear drum
Suspension
Front: Independent MacPherson strut
 with coil spring
Rear: Independent MacPherson strut
 with coil spring
Body style
Three-door hatchback
Two-door sedan
Five-door wagon 1975
Dimensions
Length: 150 in.; 159.9 in. wagon
Width: 59 in.; 59 in. wagon
Height: 52 in.; 59 in. wagon
Instruments
Speedometer
Fuel
Water
Tachometer in five-speed hatchback

Second-generation Civic four-door sedan. Second-generation Civic hatchback.

Civic, second generation 1980–83
Civic, DX, GL, S, four-door, wagon
Engine type
Standard and DX: 1335 cc

CVCC
Water-cooled
Four cylinder
Single overhead camshaft
DX, GL, S, four-door and wagon: 1488
 cc
CVCC

119

Water-cooled
Four cylinder
Single overhead camshaft
Transmission 1980–81
Standard: Four-speed manual
DX, GL, four-door and wagon: Five-
speed manual
Optional two-speed Hondamatic
Transmission 1982–83
Standard: Four-speed manual
DX, GL, four-door and wagon: Five-
speed manual
Optional three-speed fully automatic
S came only with five-speed manual
Brakes
Front disk
Rear drum
Suspension
Front: Independent MacPherson strut
with coil spring

Rear: Tubular axle, leaf springs, shock
absorbers
Sway bar on 1983 S
Body style
Three-door hatchback
Four-door sedan
Five-door wagon
Dimensions
Length: 148 in.; 160.8 in. sedan; 160.8
in. wagon
Width: 62.2 in.; 62.2 in. sedan; 62.2 in.
wagon
Height: 53 in.; 54.1 in. sedan; 54.1 in.
wagon
Instruments
Speedometer
Fuel
Water
Tachometer in DX, GL, S, sedan and
wagon

Third-generation Civic wagon.

Civic, third generation
1984–87
**Civic, DX, Si, sedan, wagon,
4WD wagon**
Engine type
Base Civic: 1342 cc
Four cylinder
Eight valve
Two-barrel carburetor
DX, Si, sedan and wagon: 1488 cc
Four cylinder
Twelve valve
Two-barrel carburetors
PGM FI on Si and 4 WD wagon
Transmission
Four-speed manual on base Civic
Five-speed manual on DX, sedan and
wagon
Four-speed automatic with lockup

torque converter optional on DX,
sedan and wagon
Six-speed manual optional on 4WD
wagon
Brakes
Power-assisted front disks
Rear drums
Suspension
Front: Torsion bar with stabilizer
Rear: Trailing link arms with beam
axle
Stabilizer bar on Si, sedan and wagon
Solid rear axle on 4WD wagon
Steering
Variable assist power rack and pinion
Body style
Three-door hatchback
Four-door sedan
Five-door wagon
Dimensions
Length: 151.4 in.; 163.2 in. sedan;
158.7 in. wagon; 160.6 in. 4WD
wagon
Width: 63.9 in.; 63.9 in. sedan; 63.9 in.
wagon; 63.9 in. 4WD wagon
Height: 52.6 in.; 54.5 in. sedan; 58.3 in.
wagon; 59.5 in. 4WD wagon
Instruments
Speedometer
Tachometer
Fuel
Water
Clock

Fourth-generation Civic hatchback.

Fourth-generation Civic wagon.

Fourth-generation Civic four-door sedan.

Civic, fourth generation 1988
Civic, DX, Si, LX, wagon, 4WD wagon
Engine type
1493 cc
Four cylinder
Twelve valve
Sixteen valve on hatchbacks
Dual-point FI
Multi-point FI on Si and 4WD wagon
Transmission
Five-speed manual
Four-speed automatic with electronic lockup torque converter optional
Brakes
Power-assisted front disks
Rear drums
Suspension
Front: Independent double wishbone with stabilizer bar
Hydraulic shocks on sedan and wagons

Rear: Independent double wishbone with gas pressurized shocks
Gas pressurized shocks on Si front and rear
Steering
Variable assist power rack and pinion
Body style
Three-door hatchback
Four-door sedan
Five-door wagon
Dimensions
Length: 156.1 in.; 166.6 in. sedan; 161.7 in. wagon
Width: 65.6 in.; 65.9 in. sedan; 66.5 in. wagon
Height: 52.5 in.; 53.5 in. sedan; 57.9 in. wagon; 58.6 in. 4WD wagon
Instruments
Speedometer
Tachometer
Fuel
Water
Clock

121

First-generation CRX.

CRX, first generation 1984–85
CRX HF, CRX, CRX Si
Engine type
1448 cc
Four cylinder
Eight valves on CRX HF
Twelve valves on CRX, CRX Si
PGM FI on CRX Si

Transmission
Five-speed manual
Four-speed automatic with lockup
    torque converter optional on midline
    CRX
Brakes
Power-assisted front-wheel disks
Rear drums
Suspension
Front: Compact strut with torsion bar
Rear: Trailing link with beam axle
Rear stabilizer bar on midline CRX
    and CRX Si
Body style
Three-door coupe
Dimensions
Length: 144.7 in.
Width: 63.9 in.
Height: 50.8 in.
Instruments
Speedometer
Tachometer
Fuel
Water
Clock

Second-generation CRX.

CRX, second generation 1986–87
CRX HF, CRX, CRX Si
Engine type
1493 cc
1590 cc on CRX Si
All aluminum
Four cylinder
Eight valve on CRX HF
Sixteen valve on CRX and CRX Si
Multi-point PGM FI on CPX HF and
    CRX Si
Dual-point PGM FI on CRX

Transmission
Five-speed manual
Four-speed automatic with lockup
    torque converter optional on midline
    CRX
Brakes
Power-assisted ventilated front-wheel
    disks
Rear drums
Suspension
Front: Independent, double wishbone
    with stabilizer bar
Rear: Independent, multi-control
    double wishbone
Rear stabilizer bar on Si
Body style
Three-door coupe
Dimensions
Length: 147.8 in.
Width: 65.7 in.
Height: 50.1 in.
Instruments
Speedometer
Tachometer
Fuel
Water
Clock

122

CRX, third generation 1988
CRX HF, CRX, CRX Si
Engine type
1590 cc
Four cylinder
Eight valve
Sixteen valve on CRX and CRX Si
Multi-point FI on CRX HF and CRX Si
Dual-point FI on CRX
Transmission
Five-speed manual
Four-speed automatic available on
  CRX midline
Brakes
Front disks
Rear drums
Suspension
Independent double wishbone
Stabilizer bar
Body style
Three-door coupe
Dimensions
Length: 147.8 in.

Third-generation CRX.

Width: 65.7 in.
Height: 50.1 in.
Instruments
Speedometer
Tachometer
Fuel
Temperature

First-generation Accord hatchback.

First-generation Accord four-door sedan.

Accord, first generation 1976–83
Engine type
1600 cc
Four cylinder
Water-cooled
Overhead camshaft
CVCC
Transmission
Five-speed manual
Two-speed Hondamatic
Three-speed fully automatic 1981
Brakes
Power-assisted front disks
Rear drums
Suspension

Front: Independent MacPherson strut
  with coil spring
Rear: Independent MacPherson strut
  with coil spring
Body style
Three-door hatchback
Four-door sedan 1979
Dimensions
Length: 162 in.
Width: 63.8 in.
Height: 52.6 in.
Instruments
Speedometer
Tachometer
Fuel
Water

Second-generation Accord four-door sedan.

Accord, second generation 1984–87

Engine type
1800 cc
Four cylinder
Water-cooled
Overhead camshaft
Twelve valve
CVCC

Transmission
Five-speed manual
Three-speed fully automatic
Brakes
Power-assisted front disks
Rear drums
Suspension
Front: Independent MacPherson strut
    with coil spring
Rear: Independent MacPherson strut
    with coil spring
Body style
Three-door hatchback
Four-door sedan
Dimensions
Length: 162 in.
Width: 63.8 in.
Height: 52.6 in.
Instruments
Speedometer
Tachometer
Fuel
Water
Clock

Third-generation Accord coupe.

Third-generation Accord hatchback.

Accord, third generation 1986

DX, LX, LXi, SEi

Engine type
1955 cc
Four cylinder
Twelve valve
Overhead camshaft
Double overhead camshaft on LXi and
    SEi sedans
Two-barrel carburetor
Multi-point PGM FI on DX coupe, LXi
    and SEi
Transmission

Five-speed manual
Four-speed automatic with lockup
    torque converter optional
Brakes
Power-assisted front disks
Rear drums
Four-wheel disks on SEi
Suspension
Front: Independent double wishbone
    with stabilizer bar
Rear: Independent double wishbone
Rear stabilizer bars on LXi and SEi
Steering
Variable assist power rack and pinion

Third-generation Accord four-door sedan.

Body style
Two-door coupe
Three-door hatchback
Four-door sedan
Dimensions
Length: 179.7 in.
Width: 67.4 in.

Height: 53.4 in.
Instruments
Speedometer
Tachometer
Fuel
Water
Clock

Prelude, first generation 1979–82

Engine type
1800 cc
Four cylinder
Water-cooled
Overhead camshaft
CVCC
Transmission
Five-speed manual
Two-speed Hondamatic
Three-speed fully automatic 1981
Brakes
Power-assisted front disks
Rear drums
Suspension
Front: Independent MacPherson strut
  with coil spring
Rear: Independent MacPherson strut
  with coil spring
Body style
Two-door coupe

First-generation Prelude.

Dimensions
Length: 161.4 in.
Width: 64.4 in.
Height: 51 in.
Instruments
Speedometer
Tachometer
Fuel
Water
Clock

Second-generation Prelude.

Prelude, second generation 1979–82
Prelude, Si
Engine type
1829 cc
1955 cc on Si
Four cylinder
Water-cooled
Overhead camshaft
Twelve valve
CVCC on base Prelude
Dual carburetors

PGM FI on Si
Transmission
Five-speed manual
Four-speed automatic with lockup
  torque converter
Brakes
Power-assisted four-wheel disks
Suspension
Front: Upper wishbone, lower lateral
  links, compliance struts, tube
  shocks, anti-roll bar
Rear: Chapman struts, lateral arms,
  trailing arms, tube shocks, anti-roll
  bar
Body style
Two-door coupe
Dimensions
Length: 161.9 in.
Width: 66.5 in.
Height: 51 in.
Instruments
Speedometer
Tachometer
Fuel
Water
Clock

Third-generation Prelude.

Prelude, third generation 1983
S, Si
Engine type
1958 cc
Four cylinder
Overhead camshaft
Double overhead camshaft on Si
Twelve valve
Sixteen valve on Si
Dual CV carburetors
Multi-point PGM FI on Si

Transmission
Five-speed manual
Four-speed automatic with lockup
  torque converter optional
Brakes
Power-assisted four-wheel disks
Suspension
Front: Independent double wishbone
  with stabilizer bar
Rear: Independent double wishbone
  with stabilizer bar
Steering
Variable assist power rack and pinion
Steer-angle dependent four-wheel
  steering optional on Si
Body style
Two-door coupe
Dimensions
Length: 175.6 in.
Width: 67.3 in.
Height: 49.2 in.
Instruments
Speedometer
Tachometer
Fuel
Water
Clock

Acura Legend

Acura Legend

Engine type
2700 cc
V-6
Water-cooled
Twenty-four valve

Transmission
Five-speed manual
Four-speed automatic

Brakes
Power-assisted four-wheel disks
Optional anti-lock

Suspension Sedan
Front: Independent, double wishbone
with coil springs, stabilizer bar
Rear: Independent, trailing link with
progressive rate coil springs,
stabilizer bar

Suspension Coupe
Front: Independent, double wishbone
with coil springs, ball-joint mounted
stabilizer bar
Rear: Independent, trailing link with
progressive rate coil springs,
stabilizer bar

Body style
Two-door coupe
Four-door sedan

Dimensions
Length: 189.4 in. sedan; 188 in. coupe
Width: 68.3 in. sedan; 68.7 in. coupe
Height: 54.7 in. sedan; 53.9 in. coupe

Instruments
Speedometer   Water
Tachometer   Clock
Fuel

Acura Integra three-door.

Acura Integra

Engine type
1600 cc
Four cylinder
Double overhead camshaft
Sixteen valve

Transmission
Five-speed manual
Four-speed automatic with lockup
torque converter

Brakes
Power-assisted four-wheel disks

127

Suspension
Front: Independent with torsion bars, struts, stabilizer bars
Rear: Semi-independent, beam-type axle, trailing link, Panhard rod, stabilizer bar

Body style
Three-door coupe
Five-door sedan

Dimensions
Length: 168.7 in.; 171.5 in. five-door
Width: 65.6 in.; 65.6 in. five-door
Height: 52.9 in.; 52.9 in. five-door

Instruments
Speedometer
Tachometer
Fuel
Water
Clock

Acura NS-x.

Acura NS-X

Engine type
3000 cc
V-6
Water-cooled
Four camshafts
Twenty-four valve

Transmission
Five-speed manual
Four-speed automatic transaxle

Brakes
Power-assisted four-wheel ventilated disks with anti-lock

Suspension
Fully independent aluminum double wishbone all around

Body style
Two-door coupe
Removable glass roof panel

Dimensions
Length: 169.9 in.
Width: 70.9 in.
Height: 46.1 in.

Instruments
Speedometer
Tachometer
Fuel
Water
Oil
Clock